BREAKING THE STRANGLE HOLD: THE LIBERATION OF GRENADA

Col Chas Dennford

Pipe Creek, TX

9 nov 85

Other books published by
Gun Owners Foundation

*The Militia in Twentieth Century America:
A Symposium* (January, 1985)

BREAKING THE STRANGLE HOLD: THE LIBERATION OF GRENADA

Frank Aker
Morgan Norval

Gun Owners Foundation

Published by
Gun Owners Foundation
5881 Leesburg Pike
Falls Church, Virginia 22041

"I understand that you love freedom, but in our crowded world you have to pay a tax for freedom. You cannot love freedom just for yourself and quietly agree to a situation where the majority of humanity over the greater part of the globe is being subjected to violence and oppression."

Alexandr Solzhenitsyn
July 9, 1975

This book is dedicated to those who paid the ultimate tax for freedom on Grenada.

TABLE OF CONTENTS

PREFACE

One week before the Grenadian army assassin-
ated Prime Minister Maurice Bishop, the militia was
disarmed. The army considered the militia to be
loyal to the government of Prime Minister Bishop.

By way of contrast, the Soviets have never been
able to disarm the Afghan people, and sidearms and
rifles at first were all that was needed to bog the invaders down into a war of attrition.

But Afghanistan is another book for which the final
chapter on citizen resistance has yet to be written.

Grenada had an ultimately happy outcome, but
no thanks to the disarmed populace. The dramatic
events of Grenada during the fall of 1983 give us food
for thought in the United States. These events may
help us evaluate the importance of the right to keep
and bear arms in the U.S. Constitution, and for that
purpose, Gun Owners Foundation is pleased to
make possible the publication of this book.

Larry Pratt
Executive Vice-President
Gun Owners Foundation

STRANGLE HOLD ON THE WORLD—
THE RUSSIAN MONGOL HERITAGE

Time: April 9, 1241. Place: Wahlstatt, near Neignitz, Silesia. Onward stormed the nimble horsemen of Prince Batu—grandson of Jenghiz Khan—and General Subadi. By dusk the Poles and Germans were in full flight westward to Austria and their commander, Duke Henry II of Silesia, lay dead on the field. The Mongols, masters of mobile, winter warfare, stood triumphant. Two days later another Tartar force surprised and crushed King Bela IV of Hungary on the plain of Mohi. Ahead, the road to the west lay open. Behind, to the east lay death and desolation; Breslay, battered; Cracow, devastated; Kiev, gutted; the Principalities of Muroum, Yaroslavl, Moscow and Kazan, ravaged. Russia, here-to-fore an intimate part of Western Europe, was cut off from Christendom by the Mongol onslaught. An Iron Curtain rang down over Eastern Europe.

In 1981, seven-hundred and forty years after the Tartar triumph at Wahlstatt the West confronts curiously, corresponding conditions. For Batu's Tartar tribesmen would settle on the Volga, take the title of the Golden Horde, and subjugate the Slavs for over two centuries. The Russians had failed to learn the lesson of 1223 when they were defeated by the forces of the Great Khan—"Emperor within the Seas"—at Kalka River. Continued disunity, in the face of a formidable foe, contributed to the demise of "Old Russia." Now, in 1241, with Eastern Europe prostrate, it was the turn of the West to tremble. But Western Europe was rent with schism between Latin and Greek, French and German, Papacy and Empire, Scandinavian and Slav, ecclesiastical and secular, spiritual and temporal, and they failed to form a united front for their own survival. Fortunately, the Mongols, after a summer interlude on the rich grasslands of Hungary, withdrew eastward to the Lower Volga, subjugating Slovenia, Croatia and Bulgaria *en route*. News of the death of the Khan at the capital of Kara Korum in far off Mongolia and the impending struggle for power, not the martial array of an awake and resolute Western Europe, probably triggered the retreat. Fate, not fortitude, had spared Christendom.

The horsemen turned eastward. But, the imprint of Tartar hooves remained stamped on the soil and soul of Mother Russia, for the Golden Horde held Moscow in subjugation for over two centuries. While the Chinese, Indians, Persians and Arabs eventually absorbed their Tartar conquerers, the Russians were mongolized.

Tribute collection and choke point control are typical Tartarian techniques. Heirs of the Khans who applied these tactics to the interior of Eur-Asia, Soviet Russia aspire to strangle the western industrial democracies by seizing the two treasure houses of the world—the petroleum laden Middle East and the mineral rich region of Southern Africa.

The danger for the West is defeat not destruction. Acting under the protective parasol of nuclear superiority, Soviet Russia in a massive Mongol Sweep is pinning the military might of NATO in Western Europe while outflanking the allies by moving into the Middle East and Southern Africa. Simultaneously the modern Mongols seek to encircle the People's Republic of China and interdict the maritime and aerial choke points of the globe upon which the Western industrialized nations depend.

Tribute collection and caravan choke point control were Mongol methods. Formidable only because of their military power, they lived by levying tribute, not by peaceful productivity. Masters of mobility and deceit, the Mongols conquered the caravan routes and commercial cross roads of Inner Eur-Asia which connected the advanced societies on the coasts of the continent.

Tartarian tactics swept almost all before the onrushing horde. Feigned rout, encirclement and flanking movements were standard maneuvers; cunning, intrigue and treachery, customary. Mobility, combined with the ability to deal with one foe at a time by radiating out of Central Asia before opponents could combine were common. The employment of trade missions and diplomatic envoys as spies, rumormongers and propagandists which prepared the path of conquest through psychological warfare were traditional Tartarian techniques. Eventually establishing a *Pax Mongolica,* which stretched from the China Sea to the Indian Ocean and on to the Mediterranean and Adriatic, the Khans, supported by grateful merchants who were granted monopolies and guaranteed secure trade routes, sought absolute security — global hegemony.

The political domination of Russia by the Mongols would only last until 1452, when Moscow signaled its assumption of the role of successor to the Golden Horde by founding a vassal Tartarian princedom in Kasimov.

The most enduring imprint of the Mongolian conquest was on the political thought of the Russian people. The Tartar state was built upon the principle of unquestioning submission of the individual to the group, first to the clan, and through the clan to the whole state. This hive principle was thoroughly impressed upon the Russian populace and it led to a system of universal service to the state. The Mongolians introduced a new concept of the power of the Prince. The Khan was absolute and autocratic. Submission was unqualified. The Dukes of Moscow, as successors to the Khans, considered their people completely subject to their will. Lands under their rule were their sole property and were devoted to the interests of the state.

The period of Tartarian domination of Russia coincided with the rise of Muscovite power. The princes of Moscow overcame their neighbors and rivals, not by the vigor with which they had attacked

the Mongol invaders, but by their success in court-
ing the Khan's favor. Muscovite princes in the four-
teenth century obtained the aid of the Tartarian armies against their Russian rivals, serving themselves
as tax-gathers and police agents for the Khans.
Aquisition of this lucrative, but debasing monopoly
enabled Ivan Kalita (1325-1341) to overtake all his
neighbors and rivals and establish a new central
Russian principality at the juncture between the
steppe and forest on the high ground between the
headwaters of the Volga, Don and Dneper. Radiating east, south, west and north, Ivan Kalita initiated
an advance under the shadow of Tartarian power
which gained even more impetus with the moving of
the Metropolitan of the Russian Church to Moscow.
This strengthened the Grand Prince's pretentions to
primacy in both spiritual and temporal affairs.

Ivan the Great (1461-1505) further amplified
Moscow's mystical mission. He took the title of Tsar
(Caesar) and assumed the mantle of the Byzantine
emperors as well as Constantinople's claim as Pro-
tector of Orthodox Christianity. The theme "Of
Romes there have been three (Rome, Constantinople, and Moscow), a fourth there will never be,"
would reverberate down the corridors of the
Kremlin which Ivan constructed. Religion—Orthodox under the Tsars and Marxist-Leninist under the
Soviets—would be wielded as a weapon in foreign
policy to win national objectives as well as an instrument of internal order to forge diverse peoples and
cultures into one through ideology. Thus, as the Tartarian threat receded, a highly centralized, authori-

tarian society based on state capitalism and ideological unity began to evolve and expand from where the forest met the steppe at Muscovy.

The oceans were their objective. Like their predatory predecessors, Atilla, Jenghiz Khan, Batu, Ulagu, Timur the Limper and Babar who had led their legions around the oceanic edge of Eur-Asia, the Russians struck out for the sea. The interior of Eur-Asia, like an inland ocean, offered no natural obstacles to expansion; neither did nature provide protection. The Ural Mountains, moved from south to north, but were low and easily traversed. Beyond, in Siberia, the ranges ran east and west cutting corridors like the Kansu pointing directly away or toward Muscovy. The rest was open steppe, first forest or *taiga* and tundra. Westward, it was the same, the Polish plains and the Baltic basin. Southward rose the Mongolian and Turkistan Uplands — easily reached, but difficult to breach, and the Caspian and Black Seas, both at the end of the three river roads — Volga, Don and Dneper running directly downriver from Moscow; while to the north lay the immobilized ocean of the Artic, open only to year around exit and entrance by way of the White Sea.

Moscow's most convenient corridors for expansion lay east and west. Moreover, only space could provide the protection not endowed by nature. Russia, if weak, would, merely serve as a parade ground for alien armies. Vast distances and military might were the only defenses. Fear of oriental onslaught, Ottoman invasion and Polish or German penetration burned deep in Moscow's memory. Moreover, these three threats from the east, south and west also offered civilization, trade and technology. They lured as well as repelled. They also opened on the ocean.

Warm water beckoned. Ever seeking the sea, the Muscovites under Ivan Kalita, Ivan the Great and their successors, Ivan the Terrible (1533-1584), along with Romanovs (1613-1917) such as Peter the Great (1689-1725), Catherine the Great (1762-1796), Alexander II (1855-1881), and Alexander III (1881-1894) pushed eastward past the Urals through Siberia and on to the Pacific (1637), southward down the river roads to the Caspian and Black Seas, westward to the Baltic and northward to the Artic. Within five centuries after Ivan Kalita the Russians had occupied almost all of inner Asia and established a trans-continental empire stretching from sea to sea.

Tsarist strategy in Inner Asia imitated the Tartars. Even tartarian tactics — winter warfare, mobility (speed and flexibility) through the use of completely mounted armies, night attacks and living off the land — prevailed until Peter the Great who introduced European military models. Russia, radiating from nuclear Moscow, thus, succeeded in conquering the caravan choke points and contacting the advanced societies which offered trade and technology. Moved by its mission the Third Rome with its tremendous population and vast area would increasingly exert a major influence on world affairs.

Objectives did not deviate after the October Revolution of 1917. The urge to warm water went on. The desire to dominate the coastal civilizations of the

continent continued. Communism replaced Ortho-
doxy as the cover for interventionism and imperialism. Internally, the Bolshevik revolution revitalized
the centralized, autocratic political system which
had decayed under the later Romanovs. Socialism
signified the recapture by the government of the economic system which had started to slip toward
private entrepreneurs. Thus, Nocolai Lenin
(1917-1924) and Joseph Stalin (1926-1953) loom as a
later day Ivan Kalita and Ivan the Great who re-
established the old order — a totalitarian, centralized
system of state capitalism bound together by ideological unity and impelled to expand by ancient im-
pulses inherited from Tartarian traditions. Muscovite, Romanov and Marxist Russia pursued the
same policies; protection through the acquisition of
space; control of the commercial caravan routes running through Eur-Asia which, until the age of sail,
connected the coastal cultures; and, since 1959,
domination of the exterior Sea Lines of Communication (SLOC) and Aerial Skyways of Transport and
Resupply (ASTAR) which serve the same purpose;
and, above all containment or envelopment of the
eternal threat out of the orient. So both tsar and
commisar strove for sovereignty in inner Eur-Asia
(Heartland), suzerenity by satellization or
neutralization (Finlandization) of the coastal cresent
(Rimland) including China, or isolation of China by
envelopment. Thus, the USSR with its emphasis on
military superiority, mobility and movement abetted
by diplomatic missions dedicated to subversion and
psychological warfare is a continuum of the Mongol

conquest and a rational replacement for the Golden Horde.

The cultural impact of the Mongol conquest on the Russian people—the dominant group, although a minority, in the USSR—is undeniable. This Tartar influence extended, in addition to ingrained political and strategic concepts, to techniques of subversion and submission.

An essential element of Mongol planning was its intelligence system. Operational plans were based on study and evaluation of amazingly complete and accurate information. The Mongol intelligence network spread throughout Europe and Asia; its thoroughness excelled all others of the Middle Ages. Spies generally operated under the guise of merchants or traders. In this, they found the Venetians quite willing to sacrifice the interests of Christian Europe in order to gain an advantage over their great trading rivals, the Genoese. In return for mongol help in ousting the Genoese trade centers in the Crimea, the Venetians acted as part of the espionage service of the Mongols.

Regarding the Russians, the KGB is the world wide intelligence gathering organ of the Russian power elite. Although no specific information is available, it would follow that certain multi-international corporations might be willing to act as the Venetians to obtain monopolistic trade advantages and access to cheap, slave labor. A peaceful, profitable world, so desired by some, under a *Pax Sovietica,* would in reality be a tyranical, tribute exacting *Pax Mongolica.*

The real war is for the minds of men. Propaganda is a weapon. The Mongols were particularly adept at psychological warfare. Tales of their ruthlessness, barbarity, and slaughter of recalcitrant foes were widely disseminated in a deliberate propaganda campaign to discourage resistance by the next intended victim. The aim was to bring about surrender by paralyzing resistance through terror. There was considerable truth in this "carrot and stick" propaganda approach. Those who resisted were annilated but the Mongols were equally most solicitous in their treatment of any foe who gave evidence of willingness to cooperate, particularly those who had skills of use. Today we see a unique world-wide effort by the USSR to subvert the nations of the globe with the threat of military pressure by exploiting the acts of brutality of the indigenous governments. This has lead the way for "national armies of revolution." Subversion has become a media event with the press carrying unwillingly the banner of Communism.

Deception is similar to both Mongol and Russian military nomenclature. The Mongols used any means to gain military and political ends. The word "horde" instead of army denoted a vast number — in reality the Mongol army was based on quality not quantity. In Russia the word "army" referres to a western equivalent of a corps of 2-3 divisions.

The exercise of hegemony over vassal states is common to both the Khans and the Kremlin. The Mongols, although small in number, positioned their capital in areas of strategic importance. They would collect tribute (usually 10% of everything) from vassal states. In return the vassal states were allowed to run their own affairs (satellitization and Finlandization). The Russians control many nations from which they extract food and consumer goods to supply their own people. Their control is indirect military clout with most nations having small Russian or Russian backed garrisons for visibility sake. Each country has its own government and is allowed to pursue national objectives as long as it turns-to when the Russians tell them to. Increasingly obvious is the taking of strategic land, air and water choke points of the world to extend its influence to other countries either directly or through isolation such as in China, and Southern Africa and U.S.

Tartar and Russian brutality are legendary. The Mongols would kill entire populations if they did not surrender upon demand: would destroy armies — not just defeat them. Thus, the conquered territories were totally safe. To keep order, they would make periodic sweeps through vassal states and kill, loot and burn for no other reason than to remind the states who is in charge. This produced a paralyzing effect due to terror. In order to expand Russian populated lands the USSR murdered between 18 and 30 million non-Russians in surrounding territories from 1917. To remind the people who was in charge, Stalin had purges periodically. Today the KGB is continually active reminding the people who is the boss. In war, the Russians are not known for their mercy and use strategy to encircle and destroy a foe.

Neither the Mongol nor Russian empires are

noted for their productivity. The Mongols were warriors and tax collectors—little or no agriculture or other production. The same is true for the Russians. Production is only a fraction of population and resource availability. The "curse" of Communism is, of course, the inability to grow enough food. The Soviets must rely, therefore, on a mighty war machine so they can, in Tartar fashion, collect tribute in the form of food, technology and industrial goods from the former Free World. Hence, both the Mongols and the Russians have attained global power by military prowess, not productivity.

The Khans employed the churches as instruments of submission. The Mongols supported and protected the churches and religion flourished. In return, the church preached acquiessence to Tartar domination. The Soviets have also employed the churches as instruments of subversion in expanding revolutionary warfare. Latin America is the most obvious example where both the Catholic and Protestant Churches have aided the leftists by preaching Liberation Theology. As the Soviet star rises some churches are seeking the protection of the Presidium. Rome, having learned during the Hungarian Uprising of 1956 that the alliance between American power and Catholic politics which saved Western Europe after World War II was ending, prepared to go underground and accomodate the modern Mongols with Vatican II. Hence, Liberation Theology, which is designed to act as a buffer between the Church and the Communists. Marxist-Leninism has, however, rarely suceeded unless imposed by force or the threat of force, and here again there is a striking similarity between Mongol Military techniques and the tactics of the Soviet Armed Forces.

Red Army Marshal M. Tuckhachevsky reintroduced Tartarian tactics to the Red Army. Tuckhachevsky, hero of the Civil and polish Wars of 1918-1920, supressor of the Kronstat Rebellion of 1921 and re-organizer of the Red Army in 1935-36, although liquidated by Stalin in 1937, left an indelible mark on the modern Soviet military mind. Dual command, ideological and military, like Prince Batu and General Subadi at Wahlstatt in 1241, was reinstated. A Communist Party commissar oversees the officers handling the troops. In Mongol and Tsarist times the emperor retained supreme military command, a position now held by the Chairman of the Presidium who also heads the Defense Council. The Tartars, moreover, initiated training of their youth for combat at the age of three or four years. Soviet primary schools begin preparing the students for eventual induction as Pioneers. This comparable command and training structure is implemented by detailed General Staff planning. The *modus operandi* of the Mongol and Soviet staff systems are similar. The strategy, tactics and logistics for every Tartar campaign was prepared in painstaking detail in advance to attain an objective defined by the Khan or Prince. In Soviet Russia, the military is relegated to the role of developing a strategy that guarantees victory. The generals are responsible for planning and do so in great detail, many times to the extent of thwarting individual initiative. Another tartarian technique is to pre-test the enemy, such as the great raid into Russia by Jenghiz Khan in 1223 which resulted in the Russian defeat at Kalka River. These extensive reconnaissances in force gathered information about foes, weapons, tactics and strength prior to the actual invasions of China, Russia, Eastern Europe and the Middle East. The Russians tend also to test an adversary's strength on foreign battlefields. For example, the Nazis in Spain prior to World War II, and the United States in Korea, Indo-China and in the various Arab-Israeli conflicts. The current proving ground in preparation for the Final Offensive is Afganistan, for the Afgans somewhat represent the U.S. in respect to war experience — independent small unit action and capabilities although lacking U.S. technology. Pre-testing of potential hostile forces, aided by intelligence, espionage and psychological warfare, enabled both the Khans and the Communists to employ their hordes in the most favorable fashion and to utilize one of their major advantages — mobility.

Speed and flexibility were the hallmarks of Mongol military movements. All of the horde was mounted. Approach marches were screened by an advance guard. These forward forces, though light on logistics and firepower, permitted the main body to mass, achieve local superiority, and break through. This gave the prince and field commander the geographical advantage of choosing the ground, the psychological superiority of surprise and the ability to concentrate the mass at the critical point.

These three techniques—ground, surprise and local superiority—have been adopted by the Soviet General Staff through the use of rapid road march and deployment of vehicles such as tanks and armored personnel carriers (APC) which follow a lightly armed, flexible advance echelon. This mode is enhanced by the organization of Soviet ground forces which are smaller and lighter than Western counterpart units and are assigned about one half of NATO frontage. Mongol mobility models are also reflected in Russian battlefield tactics.

The classic Mongol Sweep calls for holding the enemy in front by direct assault while enveloping the adversary by a flanking attack: a frontal attack to fix and a flanking sweep to enfold. Once in the rear, Tartar cavalry would strike deep, by-passing strong points for the siege train to reduce, while riding down enemy infantrymen who tended to break when outflanked. If the enemy held, then Mongols in front would feign retreat and as the adversary stormed forward, ambush the then uncoordinated main body. All of these tactics—mobility, sweep, envelopment and ambush—were ill suited for forested areas. Hence, the Tartars, like the Russians, prefer open ground and vast plains for mass movements. The Russians relearned the dangers of forested terrain in the disasterous Winter War with Finland of 1939-1940. Since 1940, the Soviets, except for partisan operations, have adhered to open ground offensives.

Wave attacks to pin, hold or even break through are common to the twin traditions. The Mongols moved forward with two lines of heavy calvary backed by three ranks of light cavalry. The light horse delivered well-aimed javelin and arrow attacks prior to the charge of the heavy horse. Similarly, Soviet ground doctrine projects two echelons of assault backed by artillery. Night attacks are not unusual. Both Tartars and Russians believe in a "twenty-four hour battlefield." Be it in the assault or marching and massing, the use of darkness for cover is common, but it is in the winter offensive that the clearest continuum of Mongol methods emerges.

The Mongols found that winter enhanced their mobility especially in crossing the frozen, deep flowing rivers of Eur-Asia. Winter warfare, especially against the West which tended to hole up during the cold months, gave the nomads increased opportunity for surprise. This was one of the major Mongol innovations, since they, like the Soviets, did not invent any new weapons, but merely, borrowed, stole or bought these system from the more advanced societies — China, India, Persia, or Western Europe, and recently, the United States — with whom they came in contact and eventually conquered.

Time: April 9, 1241. Place: Wahlstatt, near Leignitz, Silesia. Onward stormed the nimble horsemen of Prince Batu — grandson of Jenghiz Khan — and General Subadi. By dusk the Poles and Germans were in full flight westward to Austria and their commander, Duke Henry II of Silesia, lay dead on the field. The Mongols, masters of mobile, winter warfare, stood triumphant. Two days later another Tartar force surprised and crushed King Bela IV of Hungary on the plain of Mohi. Ahead, the road to the west lay open. But, the West, even in the face of this formidable foe, failed to unite. Only the death of the Great Khan in far-off Kara Korum triggered the withdrawal of the horde. Now, seven-hundred and forty years after the Tartar triumph at Walhstatt the modern Mongols stand in Silesia.

The Soviet Union, in the tartarian tradition, seeks absolute security — global hegemony. Impelled by the Three Rome Theory and true to their Mongol motherland with its mission of universal empire, Russia, having subjected numerous nationalities in Eur-Asia to satellite status and seized the caravan crossroads, is reaching out to the warm waters of the world striving to seize the choke points of the Sea Lines of Communication (SLOC) and Aerial Skyways of Transport and Resupply (ASTAR) which are vital to the Western industrialized democracies. Simultaneously, the Soviets tighten their pincers on the PRC, and in a grand Mongol Sweep, pin NATO in Europe while moving into the two oil and ore treasure houses of the world in the Middle East and Southern Africa.

Tribute collection is the objective. Finlandization is the name and *Ostpolitik* has all but brought West Germany into vassal state status. For the Soviet Union, a non-productive society with its super-power status resting on military might alone, needs the capital, technology, food and industrial plant of the western democracies to survive, specifically the Rhur and the agricultural heartland of the United States. But the Western Alliance is in disarray, torn by fear, greed and failure of faith. The time is 1981.

The place is Wahlstatt. The mongols are moving in Silesia.

> by Frank Aker and Lewis Tambs,
> current U.S. Ambassador to Columbia
> 1981

PRELUDE

The landing of a multinational force of troops from the United States and six Caribbean island nations on Grenada on October 25, 1983, suddenly thrust that tiny nation onto the center stage of world affairs.

The initial reaction was one of shock. The left-liberal faction in the United States was beside itself with indignation.

Liberal Senator Paul Tsongas (D-Ma.) bitterly questioned the invasion. He told ABC television viewers of "Nightline" on October 26, 1983, "I find it very hard to understand how an isolated community of 110,000 people can be viewed as a serious threat to those countries and to the United States."[1]

Arthur Schlesinger, Jr., raged in a Wall Street Journal Article that, "Behind the phony pretexts lies the simple fact that our president wanted to prove American power by mounting a sneak attack on a nuisance regime so weak and isolated that it could be assaulted with impunity . . ."[2]

The New York Times compared the U.S. action

in Grenada as similar to the Soviet Union's invasion in Afghanistan in 1979.

Even our allies got into the act. British Prime Minister Margaret Thatcher, apparently forgetting her own invasion of the Falklands, called the action unjustified. She added, "Western democracies cannot just march into a small country where communism reigns against the will of the people."[3]

The leftist Canadian Prime Minister, Pierre Trudeau, said he was "astonished."[4] The French government called the invasion "a surprising action in relation to international law."[5] The Socialist government of Italy said they "can only disapprove this decision,"[6] and, furthermore, the action "has dangerous precedents and also establishes another dangerous precedent."[7]

Although there was widespread liberal and media hostility to the Grenada action, the American public took a different view. Poll results indicated that 80% of those sampled approved the President's action in Grenada. They further agreed, unlike Tsongas and Schlesinger, that there were, indeed, good reasons for the action — to protect the lives of Americans on the island and to replace Marxists thugs who had shot and massacred their way into power.

The official reasons given for the action was "to restore peace and public order and respect for human rights; to evacuate those who wish to leave; and to help the Grenadians re-establish governmental institutions."[8]

As these words are written all the objectives except the re-establishment of a duly elected government have been accomplished. From a military view the Grenada action, "Operation Urgent Fury" was a success. The political fallout remains.

The Grenada incident, however, was a very important event geopolitically. It has thrown a monkey-wrench into the Soviet Union's strategic goals in Latin America.

Notwithstanding the outcries of the liberals and the media, Grenada does represent a setback for Soviet designs in Latin America. Whether the setback is temporary or permanent depends upon future action by the United States.

That action must be based on a thorough appreciation and awareness by the United States, both its decision makers and the general public, of Russian strategic plans for the area. That is the purpose of this book.

This book will explore the Soviet strategic designs in Grenada and their implications for not only the Caribbean basin, but here in the United States.

It is our contention that the Soviet's active presence in the Caribbean is a serious threat to the well being of every man, woman and child in the United States. The Soviet threat is real and how we as a nation ultimately respond to it will determine our fate as a free nation.

Notes

1. Manchester Union Leader, October, 31, 1983.
2. The Wall Street Journal, November 9, 1983.
3. The Washington Times, November 15, 1983.

4. Time, November 7, 1983.
5. Ibid.
6. Ibid.
7. Ibid.

1

GLOBAL AIMS
OF THE SOVIETS

To understand Grenada's geopolitical importance to the Soviet Union it is necessary to have a basic knowledge of the Soviet's global aims.

World War III, from the Soviet point of view, encompasses three phases, and these phases overlap in execution. They are containment, détente and double envelopment.[1]

Each cycle, or phase, lasted about twenty years. The first cycle, containment, commenced in 1946 and ended with the collapse of South Viet Nam in 1975. The second stage, peaceful coexistence, or as Henry Kissinger and the Western world call it, détente, dawned in 1960 when a U.S. Presidential Review Memorandum appeared advocating accommodation with the Soviet Union.[2] A negotiated arrangement aimed at preserving the global status quo and fostering interdependence by expanding economic trade relations with Russia emerged as American policy. U.S. efforts to reduce international tensions and to accomodate the Soviets were accompanied by unilateral U.S. disarmament and appeasement of aggression. This policy has subsequently been followed by every American administration since Johnson.

Détente collapsed for the West with Moscow's move into Afghanistan in 1979. But while the West sought a stalemate through détente, the Soviets, aided by a media compaign for peaceful coexistence, plotted their moves.

The Cuban missile Crisis of 1962 taught the Russians a hard lesson. Forced to retreat by overwhelming U.S. air, naval and nuclear power, the Russians resolved that such a reversal would be their last one.[3] They persued a policy of military buildup and exported subversion abroad.

Between 1964 and 1979, under the guise of détente, the West was retreating all over the globe. This retreat led to the collapse of the West's hard-line anti-Communist coalition. Indo-China, Angola, Mozambique, Guinea-Bissau, Rhodesia, Ethiopia, Aden, Afghanistan, Iran, Nicaragua, Grenada, Guyana and Surinam either fell directly to Marxist regimes, or became an implacable foe of the United States. In addition, the U.S. either abandoned or alienated South Korea, Taiwan, Israel, South Africa, Brazil, Argentina and Chile during this period of time.

As a result of the widening Sino-Soviet rift, the Soviets initiated the geographical encirclement of mainland China.[4] In this endeavor, they are aided by their new vassal states of Indo-China, Viet Nam, Cambodia and Laos.

During this period they accelerated their nuclear and naval armaments programs. While the West dozed through the period of détente, the Soviets were busy working to catch up and surpass the West in strength. SALT I would recognize American-Soviet nuclear parity. Salt II signifies emerging Soviet nuclear superiority.

The Soviet's goal is absolute nuclear superiority. Their already comfortable second strike capacity of 1980 was expanded to third strike capability in 1982. Their game plan is clear: Play a conventional nineteenth century colonial ground game under the protective cover of an overwhelming atomic umbrella.[5]

As early as 1973 Leonid Brezhnev announced at a Communists conference in Prague that the USSR would achieve economic, military and political hegemony by 1985. This would be so, so the Soviets think, because the third and final stage of World War III, double envelopment—surround the Peoples Republic of China and strangle the West by severing the oil and ore supplies—is well advanced and would be complete by 1985. Part of this goal is being carried out by Soviet actions in the Caribbean Region.

The Soviets actions during the containment phase seem to fit the geopolitical theories of Sir Halford Mackinder. His theory envisioned the inner reaches of Eur-Asia as the Heartland of a World Island.[6]

Containment called for a series of interlocking alliances around the Rimland or oceanic edge of the Eur-Asian continent which would isolate or check expansion from the Heartland—i.e. the Soviet Union.

Composed of peoples dependent upon sea borne transportation for their survival the Rimland, or encircling allies — SEATO (South East Asia Treaty Organization), CENTO (Central Treaty Organization), and NATO (North Atlantic Treaty Organization), along with ANZUS (Australia, New Zealand and the United States), and the Western Hemispheric partners of the Rio de Janerio Treaty — would not only cooperate in containing the Heartland/Soviet Union, but also strive to stabilize the globe by pursuing policies dedicated to free trade, private enterprise and democratic procedure.

Containment seems to be part of the Mackinder thesis which projected a world in which sea power (America and its allies) and land power (the Soviet Union and its satellites) were in continuous conflict.

In 1946 the advantage lay with the West, for Mackinder's Heartland was open to air and nuclear attack. Anglo-American navies ruled the waves, and could, hence, counter any Communist aggression along the Pacific, Indian or Atlantic shore of Eur-Asia. This state of affairs didn't last.

By trying to accomodate the Soviet Union, U.S. nuclear and naval superiority has slipped away. The alliance of advanced industrialized states was increasingly confronted with a classical pre-missile and pre-atomic strategic situation in which the USSR could employ its more advantageous geographical location and its extensive, resource laden land mass and large population against the West. The West, however, stubbornly maintained that technology could overcome historical, geographic and strategic fundamentals.

According to Mackinder's thesis, whoever controlled the interior of Eur-Asia would eventually dominate the globe.[7] He reasoned that the vast resources and interior lines of communication and supply would permit the people which populated, organized, exploited and industrialized this area would eventually enable them to strike out around the Rimland, gain access to the oceans and, by launching a blue water navy, overwhelm the surrounding sea peoples.

Mackinder's thesis was based upon a historical analysis of the success of nomadic steppe peoples from Central Asia who ravaged the rim of Eur-Asia for centuries. Attila, Genghis Khan, Batu, Ulagu, Timar the Limper and Babar led their horsemen around the oceanic edge of Eur-Asia from the China Sea, to the Indian Ocean and onto the Mediterranean and Adriatic. Stressing mobility and military might these people disdained static agricultural pursuits. Instead, these tribes were content to collect tribute from the people they had conquered.

Occasionally these tribute collecting tribes would come together into a compact mass under the disciplined, centralized command of a dynamic leader. They would then explode with brief, massive, bursts of energy, which would send them surging out of Central Asia to savage the civilizations surrounding them.

These tribes, referred to by historians as Mongols, used tactics that swept almost all before their onrushing horde. Feigned rout and flanking movement were standard maneuvers; cunning, intrigue and treachery were standard operating procedures for them. Mobility combined with the ability to deal with one foe at a time by radiating out of Central Asia before opponents could combine were common tactics. The Mongols also used the employment of trade missions and diplomatic envoys as spies, rumormongers and propogandists. These fifth-columnists often prepared the path of conquest through the clever use of psychological warfare, which was a typical Mongol technique.[8]

Masters of mobility and deceit, these nomadic Mongols conquered and controlled the caravan routes and commercial cross roads which connected the advanced societies on the coasts of the continent.

They lived by levying tribute, not by peaceful productivity. The Russians, heirs to the Mongol tradition, would attempt to apply these same techniques on inner Asia under the Tsar. They also carried on this same tradition during the twentieth century.

Since, realizing the importance of sea power, the Soviets have sought to apply Mongol tactics to the maritime world. They would attempt to use maritime mobility to effect choke point control of the Seven Seas.

Remember, that while the Chinese, Indians and Persians may have been conquered by the Mongols, they eventually absorbed them. The opposite happened to the Russians. The Russians, instead, became mongolized with a vengence. Since 1964 the Russians have moved to the sea and are applying the same time-tested Mongol techniques to the same countries on the edges of Eur-Asia by interdicting the Sea Lines of Communications rather than raiding the caravan routes with the horsemen of the Golden Horde.[9]

Since 1974, with an expanding strategic superiority, these modern Mongols have been collecting tribute from the increasingly subservient sea peoples in the form of loans, technology and food, and even slave labor from their vassal in Vietnam. The next step after this informal Finlandization would be surrender and satellization. The irony is that the West is helping bring about this final Finlandization.

Western bankers and businessmen, unable or unwilling to understand that their capital investments in the Soviet Union are hostages at the mercy of Moscow, have helped construct a military machine which will crush them in the end. These loans and sales do not give the lender or seller control over the policies of the USSR. Quite the reverse. These loans are actually are a form of hostages which the Soviets hold over the heads of Western bankers.[10] After all, the Russians already have the money. What are the bankers going to do, repossess the war machine their capital created? Fat chance the Russians will permit that! In essence then, this hostage capital and its accompanying tributary trade is merely a form of ransom paid to the Mongols (Soviets) who fully intend to exact an ever increasing levy from the West.

It is the aim of the Soviets to defeat, not destroy, the West. Tribute collection not atomic rubble is their aim. The Soviets seek to preserve the West's productive plant and agricultural output in order to prop up their own economy which has been devoted to making the USSR into the mightiest military machine on earth. The Soviet Union, like its model the Golden Horde, is a great power solely because of its military muscle. Economic, social, separatist and even religious problems abound within its boundaries. The curse of Communism is starvation and a slave-like existence. Nevertheless, aided by certain international financiers who have loaned the USSR some sixty billion dollars since 1970, abetted by many multinational corporations who have sold the Soviets advanced high-level technology, Soviet Russia is, in conjunction with national wars of liberation conducted by its Cuban mercenary stooges, seizing control of the sea lanes and strategic areas of the globe upon which the developed nations depend.[11]

Choke point control and tribute collection are Mongol tactical methods. The Soviets have suddenly emerged as a great naval power. Only a short time ago the Russian Navy was at best a coastal defense force.[12] In the past, the Soviet Union, as a self-contained energy and mineral independent land power, needed nothing more. Now Soviet task forces cruise the Sea Lanes of Communications of the Pacific, Indian and Atlantic Oceans, sea lanes which carry the oil and ore vital to the very existence of America and its allies. Even America is vulnerable, for the U.S. imports 40 percent of its petroleum and many of its strategic minerals.[13]

Most of the world seaborne commerce flows through fifteen funnels or choke points. Five inland seas—South China, Mediterranean, North, Norwegian and Caribbean; eight critical passage points—Malacca Straights, Ceylon, Horn of Africa, Mozambique Channel, Cape of Good Hope, Gibraltar and Cape Horn and Straits of Florida; along with two inter-oceanic canals — Suez and Panama; dominates the world's maritime traffic. These sea lanes link the industrialized states of the Western Pacific, Western Europe and Western hemisphere. Since 1964 the Soviets have moved quietly to expand their influence in all fifteen of these vital choke points. The Soviet-Mongols have moved to the sea with one goal: total isolation of the United States.

The sea chokepoints are the key to the geopolitical futures of the industrialized nations of the West. Cutting off the traffic in food, the "irreductible essential," might not prove fatal to those nations that have well developed agricultural bases. But stopping raw materials and the means for transferring them into usable goods are another story. In a new Cold War of global proportions the industrialized nations might have to watch while their industrial foundations, their sources of national power, erode and crumble.

A strategy that comes to grips with these realities does not have to concern itself unduly with peaceful augmentation of national assets and national power. Rather, the realistic strategy that is based on recognition of the importance of the sea and other chokepoints can and should deal with the possibility of coercive methods, including Finlandization.

One must not overlook the final two dimensions with which strategy, both the Soviets and our own, has to concern itself with. These are the air and space blankets that enshroud the earth.

DeSeversky correctly saw how the first of these would grow in importance as man gained mastery over the air dimension. However, at the same time deSeversky, a child of the air age, failed to gauge the degree to which space would become another of man's viable elements.

By implication, deSeversky projected the view that the United States would be going it alone in a future conflict. Alliances did not weigh heavily in the scale on which he calculated the possible alternatives. Somewhat more than three decades after *Air Power: Key to Survival* appeared in print, his strategy has to consider another more realistic fact. The United States cannot "go it alone" in either peace or war. A vast network of ties, including those that require the use of air lanes, links the United States to dozens of other countries in commercial, geopolitical, cultural, and other ways. In case of war, the network would eventually bind the United States and its geopolitical, political, and spiritual allies in military ways.

For convenience one can speak of Aerial Skyways of Transport and Resupply (ASTAR).[14] Partly because sea and air lanes gravitate of necessity to similar junction and transit points. Sea Lanes of Communication (SLOC) and ASTAR broadly correspond. Thus the world's fifteen sea funnels have their counterparts in the air. But the air over the north-mid Atlantic, north-mid South Pacific and the Poles accommodates seven additional skyways. Fifteen sea chokepoints become twenty-two air chokepoints.[15]

Today's realities effect strategic theory. Evidence that the Soviet Union recognizes the importance of the air chokepoints has already surfaced. The Soviets, for example, have a *Kiev*-class Vertical Takeoff or Landing (VTOL) carrier based in Cam Ranh Bay, Vietnam.[16] In a matter of days, this ship could sit astride one of the airlanes in the Pacific. The Soviet's three other *Kiev*-class carriers could be deployed in the Atlantic. These carriers would pose a potential threat to the customary northern commercial air path from New York to Europe and to "the alternative southern route from Miami, Atlanta, and New York north of the Azores and Morocco."

Planning a counter-strategy has to recognize that the air dimension also provides the road to space.

"High Frontier" is the name given to the layers of space that lie around the earth.[17] Strategically, the High Frontier may pose the United States' gravest problem or become its saviour. The decisions made today could well make it possible for the Free World to "escape the brooding menace of 'balance of nuclear terror' doctrine by deploying defensive systems in space." Failure to "look to outer (or inner) space for employment of its nuclear strategy"[18] may mean that the nation is surrendering the opportunity to defend itself militarily.

The Soviets are not ignoring space. They are going full speed with their military space program for they well realize the critical importance of a strategic presence in space.

High Frontier strategy has been talked about by many. Essentially, as presented by retired USA Gen. Daniel O. Graham, it envisions a layered defense system focused on what the authors term Space Interdiction of Communication and Missiles

(SICAM). The system would include "an antimissile defensive ring around U.S. missile silos which would destroy incoming missiles one mile away from their targets . . . ; a network of 432 satellites orbiting the earth, each of which would be able to fire 40 to 50 heat-seeking rockets . . . ; and . . . advanced (killer) satellites, which would shoot down missiles midway in their flight path."[19]

To pinpoint space chokepoints an imaginary line drawn over that part of the Earth's surface that lies directly between the territories of the United States and the Soviet Union provides an initial clue. As General Graham has observed, such identifiable sectors of space would provide the most likely ICBM attack routes. The importance of the northern polar region becomes immediately apparent.

With the Soviet now becoming a blue water naval power and casting their eyes skyward into space, they can develop and exploit the third phase of their strategic offense against the West the double envelopment phase.

The fall of Siagon in April of 1975, followed by most of Indo China ended the containment phase and nearly completed the geographical encirclement of the People's Republic of China. This has heightened and endangered the oil and ore route through the South China Sea to Japan from Iran, Arabia, South Africa and South America.[20]

Mainland China, an ancient adversay of the Soviet-Mongols, is increasingly ringed with Soviet power. A crescent of Russian bases, satellites and allies curves west, south and east around mainland

China from the Sea of Japan to the South China Sea. Shikotan, Sakhalin, Sikhote Alin, the Democratic People's Republic of North Korea, Mongolia, Siberia, Afghanistan, India and Indochina form a semi-circle around China. It starts at the Tartar Strait and closes at Cam Ranh Bay. To the south only two gaps remain along this hostile perimeter, pro-China Pakistan—threatened by a Baluchistan uprising with Soviet help—and neutralist Burma—under guerrilla attack in the north—provide Peking with uncertain avenues to the Indian Ocean and the maritime nations of the Western Alliance.

To the west, dominated by Soveit carrier battle groups operating from Vietnamese ports, lies the South China Sea—oriented south of the Nationalist Chinese held island of Taiwan. To the north—from Taiwan to South Korea lies the East China Sea and Mainland China's only access route to western technology, food and goods. Without these items Balkanization of China can begin in short order. It is ironic but the Nationalist Chinese's control of the East China Sea would become the cornerstone to the mainland Peoples Republic of China's survival.

Understandably, the Communist Chinese would like to gain control of Taiwan. We need the Communist Chinese to bleed off Russian strength. But we must also be in a position to control the Communist Chinese should they become more of a threat to the United States than Russia. The trump card to maintain this delicate balance of power is the absolute guaranteed protection of Nationalist China by the United States. In this way we not only back our

and the Mediterranean to Western Europe began to be shipped southward in super tankers along East Africa, through the Mozambique Channel, around the Cape of Good Hope and up to the South Atlantic, past Angola and Guinea-Bissau, to NATO and the United States. The world was turned upside down; the globe inverted. Hostile ports-of-call replaced friendly naval facilities.

The ultimate objective of the Soviet Union is to establish a global Communist Commonwealth.[22] Heirs of the Mongols and adhering to the Three Rome theses — "Of Romes there have been three (Rome, Constantinople and Moscow), a fourth there will never be"[23] — the Russians are employing a traditional Mongol strategy of chokepoint control, tribute collection and double envelopment in their drive for world domination.

The Soviet-Mongols have moved to the sea and are seeking to Finlandize the western industrialized nations by seizing the strategic resources upon which these advanced societies depend.

During the first two stages of Soviet World War III strategy — cold war and détente — the Soviets built a massive nuclear and naval machine.[24] The current phase of their World War III thinking, double envelopement, is directed at encircling the peoples Republic of China and denying the West access to oil and ore. The oil of the Middle East and the ore of Southern Africa are their immediate objectives. Loss, or denial of access to either one of these areas will cause the collapse of Western Europe and Japan and endanger the very existence of the United States.

Southern Africa is a storehouse of strategic minerals. Many of the minerals — chrome, cobalt, scr- manganese, nickel, vanadium, and titanium — are only duplicated in commercial quantities in the Soviet Union or in the Communist Commonwealth.[25] Thus, satellization of Southern Africa would enable the Soviet Union to establish a communist mineral cartel which could control the West through control of essential mineral supply. The Republic of South Africa, moreover, monitors the supertanker sea route from the Middle East. They run southward through the Indian Ocean along the East African coast through the Mozambique Channel and around the Cape of Good Hope before angling northward into the Atlantic Ocean. They then travel past Namibia (South West Africa), Angola and Guinea-Bissau to terminate in the United States and Western Europe.

Thus, the independence of Southern Africa and the reintegration of South Africa into the Western alliance is essential to Western survival.

The Soviets have moved to isolate South Africa. Angola, Zambia, Zimbabwe and Mozambique have all fallen to Soviet backed forces. South Africa now faces the task of surviving the continued onsloughts from both within and without. The way is now open for the final attack on the U.S. This can be made through its strategic rear, the Caribbean region.[26]

With the Soviet's global game plan in mind let us examine how it applies to the Caribbean region and one tiny island located in it.

Notes

1. Lewis A. Tambs "World War III: The Final Phase—Finlandization" Vital Speeches Vol. 47, p. 154.
2. Ibid., p. 155
3. Senator Jesse Helms "Soviet Expansion in Central America and the Caribbean Basin" Congressional Record Vol. 129; April 25, 1983. S. 5233-37
4. "The Caribbean," Intelligence Digest 18 June 1980 p. 2.
5. Ibid., p. 2
6. Sir Halford Mackinder "The Geographical Pivot of History" Geographic Journal. London, Vol. 23, 4 (April 1904) p. 436.
7. Tambs, "World War III" p. 155.
8. Lewis Tambs and Frank Aker, "Khan, Kremlin and Commisar: From the Pax Mongolica of 1241 to Pax Sovietica of 1981." Futurable (Argentina) Vol. 11, May 1981, p. 40. 9. Ibid.
10. Bertram D. Wolfe, "A Life in Two Centuries" (New York: Stein and Day, 1981), p. 166.
11. Shmauel Katz, "The Flawed Architect," Jerusalem Post, 12 October 1979.
12. "How the Soviet Navy Thinks," Review of the News, December 14, 1983, p. 45.
13. Margaret Daly Hayes, "United States Security Interests in Central America in Global Perspective" Central America: International Dimensions of the Crisis, Ed. by Richard E. Fienberg (New York, Holmes & Meier, 1982)., p. 91.
14. Frank Aker, "Geopolitics of WW III in Central American and the Caribbean" U.S. Army War College Military Policy Symposium 21-23 Nov 82, p. 5.
15. Ibid. p. 5
16. "Soviet Global Power Projection" Soviet Military Power, Department of Defense 1981, p. 93.
17. Tom Nugent "Movement Towards High Frontier" Washington Times. November 1, 1983, p. 2B.
18. Ibid.

19. Ibid.
20. Lewis A. Tambs "Guatemala, Central America and the Caribbean." Congressional Record, Vol. 128, 25 February 1981, p. SL211.
21. Tambs "World War III" p. 156.
22. Tambs and Aker, "Khan, Kremlin and Commisar" p. 45.
23. Ibid.
24. Albert L. Weeks and William C. Brodie "Global Ambitions of the Soviet State" War and Peace: Soviet Russia Speaks (National Strategy Information Center Inc. New York, 1983) p. 32-33.
25. Edward A. Lynch "Bold Action In Grenada: Countering A Soviet Threat" The Heritage Foundation Backgrounder, Washington D.C. Oct 26, 1983, No. 303 p. 6.
26. Jiri Valeuta, "Soviet Strategy in the Caribbean Basin, Proceedings Naval Review 1982, p. 169.

2

THE BEAR IN
THE CARIBBEAN

The current crisis in the Caribbean is the result of the grand geopolitical game plan of the Soviets — a dagger at the throat of the United States. For the United States, the Caribbean not only constitutes a protective southern border but is also the source of valuable transit points upon which the economic survival of the United States depends.

Though the level of attention focused on the region has varied over the years, the assumption that the United States has security interests in the region has never been questioned by most rational thinking people. However, the growing reality is that the politically quiescent Caribbean Region is changing from a friendly buffer zone to an enemy military staging base. The United States is being outflanked!

Russia's intentions in the Western Hemisphere were made quite clear as early as 1924 when the Soviet Commissar for Foreign Affairs, Yuri Chicherin, announced that Mexico City had been selected as the headquarters for the activities of the Communist International in Latin America. The 1966 meeting of the Non-Aligned Tri-Continental Congress in Havana, with Soviet officials orchestrating the strategy, Cuban leaders arranged for pro-Soviet guerrilla leaders from Central America to meet with representatives of a new (2-year old) instrument of world terrorism the PLO.[1] A Cuban-PLO-Central American axis was born. This unholy alliance agreed in 1969 in a meeting in Mexico to cooperate in the "mutual struggle against U.S. imperialism."[2]

Money, weapons, medicinal supplies, training, etc., were to be made available for use in Nicaragua, El Salvador, and Honduras by the USSR, Cuba, Libya, North Korea, Vietnam, and the PLO.

By 1980, after 14 years of plotting and fighting, Communist forces, with the help of sympathetic groups, subdued Nicaragua. That present government is now the principal Soviet and Cuban instrument for the job of Communizing the rest of Central America. El Salvador is now under attack. While the U.S. and the West twiddle their thumbs and sit around debating the issue "Why should we defend El Salvador," arms are pouring into the arsenals of the pro-Soviet forces. While this hand-wringing is going on, Salvadorans are defending themselves against increasing odds from a Marxist take-over. El Salvador, one should realize, is America's present line of resistance against Soviet pretentions for the U.S. itself.

If we take communism seriously (and why shouldn't

we, look at how much of the globe is under their control), then we must take seriously their ultimate goals — Communist global hegemony.[3] Instead, we are being constantly told by liberals and Marxist appologists that these are socialist states trying to right past injustices. Instead of righting injustices, however, these socialist states have placed their people under a harsh totalitarian form of slavery. Despite Soviet disinformation claims to the contrary,[4] a new socialist order is always more repressive than the government it replaced.

These new socialist states have suddenly become focal points of increasing Soviet military activity in the territory of their neighbors.[5]

To help project their power in the Caribbean, the Soviets have suddenly emerged as a great naval power.

The Soviet Navy has the task of denying the U.S. its strategic oil and industrial minerals and to gain control over the worlds sea routes. Admiral of the Soviet Fleet Gorshkov writes: The Soviet Navy is an instrument of a peace-loving policy and the friendship of peoples, a policy of suppressing the aggressive aspirations of imperialism, detering military ventures and resolutely counteracting threats to the security of the peoples on the part of imperialist powers.

"With the appearance of the Soviet Navy on the ocean expanses, the Soviet Union has been given new, wider potentialities for using the fleet in peacetime to support the country's state interests. And these potentialities are being successfully realized."[6]

Soviet task forces cruise the Caribbean. Russian

reconnaissance planes regularly fly monitoring missions from Cuba to Guinea-Bissau and back. During the past two decades, the Caribbean has been increasingly infected with a cancer that threatens to choke off the petroleum products vital to the survival of the United States of America, the keystone of the western coalition.

The United States, which is dependent on other lands for 93 out of 95 strategic minerals and which imports over 43 percent of its energy needs must realize that the Caribbean is critical to its survival.[7]

The viper in the nest vis-à-vis the United States' interest in the Caribbean is the Soviet Union's surrogate Fidel Castro.

U.S. efforts to contain Castro after the Bay of Pigs fiasco in 1961 and the promise of nonintervention concluding the Cuban Missile Crisis of the 1962 chained the U.S. to a passive policy of reaction and restraint rather than an active program of initiative and offense. This committed the United States to a defensive posture and merely enabled Moscow and Havana, not only to establish, but also to insure their sway over their subjects in the region.

In 1970, many of 1962 missile-crisis tensions returned when the Soviets sailed a submarine tender into Ceinfuegos on the island's southern coast.[8] American U-2 reconnaissance flights further revealed construction activity ashore of a type clearly connected with submarine operations. The tender departed only after the U.S. government let it be known publicly and forcefully that it viewed the tender's presence, along with the associated work

ashore, as a direct and grave violation of the agreement by which the two countries had resolved the
1962 confrontation. Construction ashore, however,
continued.

In 1972, Moscow again tested the political atmos-
phere when it ordered the first ballistic-missile-firing
submarine, a diesel powered Golf II, into Cienfuegos. The Soviet aim behind these moves was to
establish a forward operating base for the USSR's
Yankee-class, nuclear powered, strategic submarines
—similar to the American presence at Holy Loch,
Scotland and Rota, Spain.

Soviet naval units accompanied by naval aircraft
and the most modern ships in the Soviet navy had
now become routine occurrences in Cuban waters,
the Caribbean Sea, and the Gulf of Mexico. Unfortunately, no one in the United States seemed to be
much concerned about a fundamental fact of maritime life brought home by this continuing Russian
presence. From Cuban-based ports and airfields,
Soviet naval and air forces could cut all of the main
shipping routes connecting South America and
Panama with the Gulf and East Coast ports of the
United States. They could also cut those sea lanes
extending from the Panama Canal and the Gulf of
Mexico to the Harbors of Western Europe.[9]

In April of 1981, a Soviet cruiser arrived in the
port of Muriel, Havana, Cuba. The significance of
this visit completely escaped the nation's news
media. The showing of the Soviet flag in the Caribbean occurred at a time when the new administration was denouncing Cuban support of the Salva-

doran guerrilla offensive and getting cat-calls from the media for its effort. The campaign to aid El Salvador reflected Washington's desire to reassert U.S. interest into a region that had been previously neglected for so long by U.S. policy makers. The presence of the Soviet's warship was a reminder to the United States and other nations that the Caribbean is no longer an American lake, but has become a Soviet sea.[10]

The presence of Soviet naval power has now breached this traditional American bastion. It's navy has served as a direct extension of Soviet influence. The nature of Soviet naval activities in the Caribbean has been primarily to demonstrate and establish its presence. The navy has also been employed not only as a tool to demonstrate Soviet support for the Castro regime, but has shown Soviet ability to launch naval operations the Caribbean region.

Soviet naval operations were initially conducted in the region on a low profile. Merchant vessals were carrying the life blood to Cuba. They comprised the predominance of Soviet shipping from 1963 to 1968. It was this shipping which opened the Caribbean to Soviet maritime power. While these ships served as transports for equipment and material to Cuba, they also provided support for covert Cuban activities. On a limited basis, Soviet merchant ships helped Cuban fishing vessels transport weapons and personnel to guerrilla movements in Latin America. After 1968, Soviet merchant shipping has become more overt in its support of military and naval operations.[11] The same shipping which carries heavy weapons and equipment to Cuba, is now capable of supporting Soviet or Cuban amphibious landing operations because of their roll-on, roll-off capability.

Of an even more important nature is the resupply function which Soviet merchant shipping performs for Soviet warships. Merchant vessels have been used to acquire food, fuel, and water in ports which are prohibited to Soviet war ships. They would then replenish these warships at sea or in friendly ports. This allows Soviet naval vessels a greater degree of flexibility while operating at the limits of their lines of communication.[12]

Intelligence gathering in the Caribbean has been conducted by Soviet Bloc trawlers under the pretense of fishing. During the period from 1962 to 1968, the sighting of Soviet Bloc trawlers in the Caribbean averaged 25 per year. Many of these vessels lacked any noticeable evidence of fishing equipment but possessed the necessary electronics equipment to collect signals intelligence.[13] In July 1970, observation of a Soviet trawler revealed the vessel was manned by uniformed naval personnel. The trawler was operating off the coast of Cape Kennedy at the time of the Poseidon missle test firing.

It is important to note, that both the Soviet merchant and fishing fleets are subservient to the needs of the navy. They form an important cog in Soviet naval operations.[14]

The Soviets cast a covetous eye on the Caribbean shortly after Castro seized power. Cienfuegos, Cuba, was chosen to be the site of a Soviet submarine base.[15] It was built under the guise of being a sugar terminal and was completed near the end of 1970. Located approximately 50 miles east of the Bay of Pigs, the site offered the Soviets a high degree of security. The narrow entrance to the bay and the isolation of the surrounding countryside makes access to the base difficult. The base is a permanent one and is larger than the U.S. submarine base in Rota, Spain, but smaller than the one in Holy Loch, Scotland.

The base was designed to handle nuclear submarines with two 80 foot barges used for storing radioactive effluent reactor waste. The base also consists of a 200 man barracks, communication center, an anti-submarine net, and other facilities associated with Soviet submarine operations.[16]

The base at Cienfuegos has allowed nuclear powered cruise missile submarines and conventionally powered GOLF and Echo ballistic missile submarines to operate in Caribbean waters. These submarines also posses a nuclear missile capability. This would allow them to target strikes against a number of population centers in the southeastern United States.[17] It is difficult to state whether or not nuclear powered submarines of either the YANKEE or DELTA class have operated in the Caribbean. However, it is possible that at least YANKEE class submarines have conducted operations in this region.

The existence of Cienfuegos provides Soviet submarines with the capacity to remain on station 20 to 50 percent longer than previously experienced because they would not have to return to the Soviet Union for resupply or maintanence. It also provides nuclear powered ballistic missile submarines with a support base in the event of a destabilization of relations between the two super powers.

The first deployment of Soviet warships to the Caribbean occurred in July of 1969. They consisted of a missle-armed cruiser, two missle armed destroyers, three attack submarines (one nuclear powered) and three auxiliary ships. This task force introduced Soviet naval power to the Caribbean. This helped to bolster and enhance the Soviet Union's development of political power and influence in the region.[18]

On May 14th 1970, a seven unit naval squadron that included a submarine tender, arrived in Cienfuegos to re-stock supplies. After two weeks two anti-submarine warfare ships and one auxiliary ship departed Cienfuegos for Havana. The three submarines and a tender which had accompanied these vessels remained in the vicinity of Cienfuegos. A third task force consisting of mostly tankers, an oiler and a number of auxiliary ships put into Cienfuegos on September 10, 1970.[19] The composition of this squadron indicated that now Cienfuegos has the necessary equipment and material to be made completely operational. Since these initial inclusions into the Caribbean, Soviet naval forces have operated in the region with increased frequency.

There are disadvantages for Soviet naval forces operating in the Caribbean. Cuba and other third world countries in which the Soviets maintain naval bases are at the limits of Soviet lines of communication. It is also a fact of life that warships deploying from home ports in the Soviet Union must pass through NATO chokepoints. For these reasons, the Soviets have decided to begin production of major surface ships capable of sustaining themselves longer from third world bases. Surface ships with this capability would then be able to add continuity to Soviet presence in the Caribbean.

Soviet naval aircraft provide another dimension to naval operations in the region. Since 1970, the Soviets have maintained Cuban bases for BEAR-D aircraft. These are the largest aircraft in the Soviet naval air inventory and are capable of flying non-stop without refueling from Cuba to Murmansk, in the Kola Penninsula of northern Russia. BEAR-D aircraft are used for long range reconnaissance and conduct near routine flights off the U.S. Atlantic coast.[20]

The inclusion of Grenada into the Cuban camp not only increases the operating distances of Cuban/Soviet aircraft but also has other definite strategic implications. A new airport with a 10,000 foot runway under construction in Grenada was capable of supporting any existing Soviet made aircraft. The airstrip will provide Cuban transports with a guaranteed refuelling stop on their way to Africa. Of far greater importance, however, and the danger to the U.S., would have been the ability of Soviet aircraft to interdict vital oil routes in the Atlantic from this Grenada airfield.[21]

The Soviet position has been developed through the maintenance of Cuba as a representative of its strategic interests in the Western Hemisphere. The Soviets now seek to advance their naval power in the Caribbean in order to expand their sphere of influence and, more importantly, to utilize the strategic value of the region.[22]

In contrast to the Soviet's thought out goals is the lack of consensus in the United States over U.S. national interests in the Caribbean. Use of the Caribbean by Soviet naval forces now compels the west to evaluate the strategic importance of the region. This Soviet naval presence not only threatens the security of the Western Hemisphere but threatens to tip the strategic balance to the Soviets.

Soviet naval power in the Caribbean is now a reality. In its present stages it can be regarded as more political than operational. However, the Soviets seek the strategic advantage in the Caribbean. Naval developments and increases in force may provide the Soviets with certain strategic options which could influence global strategy.

The problem that faces the United States is twofold: it must regain the confidence of the nations in this region and stem the expansion of Soviet naval power.

Notes

1. R. Bruce McColm, "Central America and the Caribbean: The Larger Scenario" Strategic Review, Summer 1983, p. 35.
2. Donald S. McAlvany, "Revolution In Central America" The McAlvany Intelligence Advisor, May 1983, p. 8.
3. Albert L. Weeks and William C. Brodie "Global Ambitions of the Soviet State," War and Peace: Soviet Russia Speaks. (National Strategy Information Center Inc. New York, 1983) p. 32-33.

4. Soviet Active Measures: Forgery, Disinformation, political Operations. Special Report No. 88 Department of State October 1981, p. 1-5.

5. Jeane J. Kirkpatrick, "Central America: The Challenge On Our Doorstep." The New Force p. 9-10.

6. "Soviet Global Power Projection." Soviet Military Power, Department of Defense 1981, p. 92.

7. Frank Aker, "Geopolitics of WW III In Central America and the Caribbean." U.S. Army War College, Military Policy Symposium 21-23 November 82, p. 3.

8. Margaret Daley Hayes, "United States Security Interests In Central America In Global Perspective." Central America: International Dimensions of the Crisis, Ed. by Richard E. Fenberg (New York, Holmes & Meiery 1982), p. 90.

9. "The Caribbean," Intelligence Digest, June 18, 1980 p. 2.

10. Ibid., p. 1.

11. "Soviet Global Power Projection." p. 93.

12. Ibid.

13. George C. Wilson, "Crates of Soviet Aircraft Detected Near Havana." The Washington Post 12 January 1982.

14. "Soviet Global Power Projection," p. 93.

15. Senator Jesse Helms "Soviet Expansion In Central American and the Caribbean Basin" Congressional Record Vol 129: April 25, 1983, S. 5233-37.

16. Fred C. Ikle, "Soviet Imperialism Spreads South," Defense, March 1982 p. 26.

17. Helms, "Soviet Expansion" p. S. 5233-37.

18. McColm, "Central America And The Caribbean," p. 33.

19. Ibid.

20. Helms "Soviet Expansion" p. S. 5233-37.

21. Edward Lynen, "Moscow Eyes the Caribbean," The Heritage Foundation Background, Washington D.C. August 12, 1983, No. 284 p.4.

22. Ikle, "Soviet Imperialism," p. 26.

3

RUSSIAN SURROGATES
IN THE CARIBBEAN

The Soviet Union makes extensive use of surrogate forces to further their global policies. Soviet surrogates are used quite extensively in the Caribbean. Their main puppet is Fidel Castro's Communist Cuba.

Cuba is the key to the Caribbean. Ever since the advent of the maritime empires in the sixteenth century the Pearl of the Antilles has, by virtue of its central location, command of the Windward and Yucatan Channels along the Santaren Passage and the Florida Straits.[1]

Its relatively large size, population, agricultural potential and numerous deep water harbors, served as the strategic center of gravity in the closed, continental sea of the Caribbean.

The introduction of air and, ultimately, missile power in the twentieth century has further enhanced the island's importance. The coming to power of Fidel Castro in Cuba in 1959 and his subsequent alliance with the Soviet Union has altered the geopolitical balance in the Caribbean.

Cuban military ties with the Soviet Union and the growth of Soviet air and naval presence in Cuba pose the most significant military threat to U.S. security interests in the hemisphere.[2]

Although highly dependent upon the USSR, Cuban military forces are large, modern, and increasingly professional. Because of Cuba's proximity to vital Caribbean sea lanes, the Soviets or Cubans in wartime would attempt to cut the movement of troops, supplies, and raw material in the Gulf of Mexico or the Caribbean Sea. They could also strike key facilities in the area. Indeed, the Caribbean sea lanes are a series of chokepoints, some no more than 90 miles wide. Along with the Florida Straits, the Yucatan Channel, the Windward and the Mona Passages can all be shut-off from Cuba.[3]

Their closure can seal off America's Gulf Coast ports and interrupt most of the traffic heading to the Eastern Seaboard from the Panama Canal and South America. With Cuba a Soviet surrogate, the United States — in fact NATO since the U.S. is the major supplier of NATO — will be confronted with a direct threat to the control of the areas vital interisland bottlenecks.[4]

To enhance this threat the Soviets have in the last two years alone delivered to Cuba two billion dollars worth of military hardware totaling 131,000 tons.[5]

Cuba's military personnel strength has increased and its military capabilities have improved dramatically over the last five years.

A significant trend has been the development of

an effective ready reserve which gives Castro and his Soviet masters a well trained and, to a large extent, battle experienced mercenary force which can be activated on short notice. About 70 percent of Cuba's forces in Angola and Ethiopia are these ready reservists who were recalled to active duty.

The Cuban military capability is far in excess of any actual or imaginary defensive needs. Cuban armed forces include an army of over 225,000, a navy of about 11,000, and air and air defense forces of 16,000.[6] These figures do not include hundreds of thousands of paramilitary forces which in many instances are better trained and equipped than the regular armed forces of other Caribbean countries.

The Cuban army includes 15 active and reserve divisions. The Cubans have over 250 MIG fighter aircraft, 650 tanks, 90 helicopters, two FOXTROT attack submarines, one KONI-Class frigate, and about 50 torpedo and missile attack boats.[7]

The Cuban military has made great strides in moving from an essentially defensive force to one with offensive interdiction capability. The naval forces have been noted, but of particular concern are the new high performance nuclear capable, mach 1.5-2.0 MIG-23/27s that are now being delivered in ever increasing quantities. To protect these aircraft, Cuba has built coverite bombproof hangers and added a sophisticated air defense system over their location. The danger lies not only in their chokepoint control ability,[8] but their range is such that they can strike within minutes an arch stretching from New Orleans, Louisiana to Savannah, Georgia.

Nicaragua is another Latin American country that has fallen within the Soviet Union's orbit. As a result, the Communists have established their first major base of operations in Central America. This occurred in 1979 when they teamed up with the Cubans, the Carter Administration, and Congressional liberals to oust President Somoza and establish the Communist Sandinistas in power in Nicaragua. Today, Nicaragua is being used as the Soviet base for the communization of all of Central America from Panama through Mexico.

There are now between 7,000 and 8,000 Cuban civilian advisors and about 1,500 Cuban military and security advisors in Nicaragua. Cuban advisors are believed to be serving in key posts throughout the government. There they exert considerable influence on the Nicaraguans and, at the same time, control them so they won't stray from the Marxist line.[9]

The Cubans in Nicaragua are also getting a lot of help from their East European buddies. We may soon see more East German police advisors, those efficient nasty Gestapos that operate in South Yeman and Angola.

There are, in addition to Cuban, over 5,000 Russian, East German, Bulgarian, PLO, and other East Bloc advisors in Nicaragua. That total is now 100 times more numerous than all American military advisers in all of Central America! Their mission is to assist in building the Sandinista Army from its currently estimated strength of 60,000 into a force of 250,000. Once achieved, this military buildup will mean one in 10 Nicaraguans are under arms. Even at its present strength, the Sandanista Army represents the largest military force in the history of Central America.[10]

About 70 Nicaraguans are being trained as jet pilots in Bulgaria. Existing landing strips in Nicaragua are being lengthened and will be able to accommodate sophisticated jet aircraft. Two airfields are located on the Eastern Coast. Puerto Cabenzas in the north, on Miskito Indian lands, and Bluefields in the south. The Montelimar airfield is located near the Pacific Coast near Managua.[11]

Soviet advisors are deeply involved in directing the effort to upgrade the Nicaraguan Air Force. Although there is no evidence of MIGS in Nicaragua at present, the sighting of incoming MIG-21 crates in Cuba provides cause for concern.[12]

Arrival of MIGs would dramatically increase Nicaragua's threat to its neighbors, whose fighter inventory consists of aging World War II vintage propellor-driven and early post-WWII jet fighters. Honduras, for example, has only 20 super MYSTERE and F-86 fighters with no all-weather capability. A loss of a single aircraft will degrade this modest capability. Since Nicaragua's neighbors have no match for MIGs, one must ask why Nicaragua would want such an air buildup?

Why would Nicaragua want to maintain an Army that has over 50 T-54 tanks, 3 brigades of artillery, over 100 anti-aircraft systems, armored personnel carriers, mobile rocket-launchers and 1,200 trucks?[13] They are hell-bent on being a destabilizing force in the area is the logical conclusion one is brought to conclude.

It is important to understand the dynamics of what is going on at the outer edges of Soviet imperialism. What does the size of Nicaragua's armed forces tell us? It tells us this: if Mexico, our good friend and neighbor, were ruled by a Sandinista regime and if such a regime followed the pattern of the Sandinista military buildup, Mexico would acquire an armed force of nearly seven million men! That is what the per capita mobilization in Nicaragua would translate into for Mexico—almost two million under arms with the present Sandinista buildup, and nearly seven million with the projected Nicaragua buildup.[14]

Mexico, of course, is a free and independent democracy, with which we live in peace. Today, Mexico currently has approximately a 120,000 man military force.[15]

Mexico, however, is the key target of the Soviet's plan to isolate the United States in the Western hemisphere. Marxist terrorists and insurgency is inching its way north towards Mexico preparing it for revolution. From Nicaragua to El Salvador to Guatemala the Red tide will threaten Mexico by spreading the poison of Communist revolution.

Mexico is ripe for revolution. The makings of it "are contained in Mexico's impoverished peasantry moving into cities where they are subject to demagogic mobilization, and a political structure that has become weak, and very corrupt."[16] With inflation raging at over 100%, unemployment of 35%, a 90%

Peso devaluation in 1982, IMF enforced austerity on a nation that is nearly bankrupt, and incredible government corruption, a Mexican revolution may be just around the corner.

The biggest factor aiding a communist revolution, however, will be the giant Soviet fifth column in existence in Mexico. It should be remembered that the Cuban revolution in the 1950's was an off-shoot of a KGB plot to plunge Mexico into civil war and destroy its government by armed force. A Mexican KGB agent has since said they would make Mexico "another Vietnam."[17]

As early as 1966, KGB specialist Boris Kolomyakov was sent to Mexico to organize the revolution. Hundreds of Mexicans were recruited to attend the Patrice Lumumba University in Moscow and were trained in terrorist tactics in North Korea. Clandestine terrorist schools were established throughout Mexico. This huge Soviet underground is in place today just waiting for the order to come from Moscow to begin the revolution.

The Mexican government itself has veered sharply to the left in recent years, and has very close relations today with both Cuba and Russia. The government is a staunch supporter of the Sandinistas in Nicaragua. It is quietly supporting 30,000 terrorists who operate out of base camps in southern Mexico against Guatemala. The Mexican government has published lists of millions of Mexicans who have allegedly transferred money to the U.S.[18] — they estimate $44 billion over the past 2-3 years.

An invasion of illegal aliens from Mexico is currently underway. The Border Patrol estimates that the total number of Mexicans which sneaked into the U.S. in 1983, was about 2 million.[19] There are countless illegal Mexican aliens already in the U.S. It is estimated that about 10% of Mexico's total population of 73 million (or about 7 million) are now living illegally in the U.S.[20] If only 1% of those were radical Marxists that represents a potential fifth column of some 700,000 potential revolutionaries within our borders with more coming every day.

Mexico is the Soviets next target, right after Central America. But remember, the *ultimate* target, however, is the United States.

Nicaragua, a Soviet surrogate, is now regularly violating Honduran territory to supply the Salvadoran guerrillas. The Nicaragua military buildup is unquestionably a threat to efforts in Central America to move towards pluralism and self-determination.

From their beachhead in Nicuragua, the Soviets are supplying and directing the Marxist revolutionaries in El Salvador and laying the groundwork for the Communist march north into the United States. As a key pawn in the Soviet's geopolitical chess game, El Salvador, is an important objective in Moscow's global plan, for it borders Honduras and lies between Nicaragua and Guatemala—A Marxist El Salvador would become the new "Ho Chi Minn Trail" of Central Americe—the route which would supply weapons, and manpower from Nicaragua to the Marxist revolutionary movement in Guatemala.

A Marxist government in Guatemala would demand the return of Chiapas province which was ceded to Mexico in 1824. Why would Guatemala want Chiapas back? One word tells it all—oil, extremely rich deposits of oil. Mexico, however, has every intention of holding on to its oil-rich province. Thus, rejection of Guatemala's demand would invite the Soviets via their new puppets in the "Peoples Republic of Guatemala" to export the Marxist revolution to Mexico where its stagnant economy, rising birth-rate and a history steeped in revolution makes it an ideal target.

Once the Marxist revolution begins in Mexico the Russians can play their end game. The Communist will take advantage of our Immigration Laws and stampede the United States into destruction by running literally millions of refugees over our southern border. A revolution in Mexico would trigger provisions of the Refugee Act of 1980 and the Refugee Education Assistance Act of 1980 which would ease immigration requirements for refugees fleeing from war-torn, revolution-infested countries.

It is estimated that the 300,000 refugees, the boat people and Castro's 1980 Cuban cast-offs, cost the taxpayer, in welfare, education and other benefits, about $2 billion per year. Now imagine how these costs would skyrocket if the numbers of refugees were increased three, five or ten-fold! That is precisely what the Soviets want.

A conservative guess would be at least 10 to 12 million people might try to cross the Mexico-U.S. land bridge to flee Communist persecution and oppression. As our experience illustrates, the Rio Grande is hardly an imposing obstacle to determined people, and geographically, the impact would fall unevenly, with the southern states receiving a higher number of refugees than other regions. The resulting economic and political stress would be enormous with the American taxpayer forced to bear the financial burden of paying billions for their upkeep.

The refugees impact on the job market would also be dramatic, especially in unskilled labor positions where unemployment is already high. Where will the billions come from to take care of these refugees and the people they displace? Since raising taxes to take care of people who are causing massive unemployment isn't politically popular, the funds will in all likelihood be shifted from the Defense Department to social service agencies such as Health and Human Services. The welfare budget will climb while the defense budget is trimmed. U.S. strength vis-à-vis the Soviets will diminish with ominous hazzards. The U.S. will be forced to withdraw troops from our overseas commitments, especially NATO, for use to patrol our southern borders in a vain attempt to stem the flood of refugees into our southern states.

Although most of the refugees fleeing to the U.S. will be seeking to escape political persecution, some, no doubt, will be entering this country for the sole purpose of continuing the revolution. It is quite reasonable to assume that many trained saboteurs and Marxist provocateurs will be among the refugees fleeing north. One has to be very unrealistic to assume that all these refugees are apostles of democracy and free enterprise.

In Texas and California there is already talk of "Recongista." Indeed, thousands of Chicanos and their activist leaders say they will stop at nothing short of reclaiming California and the Southwest for Mexico.

Rudolfo Acuna, professor of Chicano studies at California State University in Northridge and author of the book "Occupied America, the Chicano Struggle for Liberation," stated in the *Chicago Tribune* that "California, Arizona, Nevada, Utah, and parts of Wyoming, Colorado and New Mexico were all stolen from Mexico by the Americans in the war of 1846, and were once known as Aztlan."[21]

He also views Texas, which won its independence from Mexico in 1836, as part of the lands taken from Mexico. "There is growing support for a full-scale separatist movement Chicanos in California and the Southwest much like the one going on right now in French-speaking Canada,"[22] Arcuna said. "If economic conditions do not improve, a Mexican separatist movement could be under way in 10 years."[23]

A flood of refugees from Mexico would escaberate the economic and political conditions. Aided by the Marxist revolutionaries infiltrating with the refugees, the hue and cry by the separatists could easily be transformed to violent revolutionary acts of sabotage and terrorism throughout the Southwest United States.

As the problems resulting from the refugee flood grows—unemployment, high taxes, social frustration, etc., many more U.S. troops will suddenly find themselves thrust into the position of maintaining order in the south and southwest cities where growing resentment and hostilities towards the refugees turn to violence.

Carlos Ferandiz, a Los Angeles Chicano activist claims, "There will be an uprising here, it is just a matter of time. We will create our own country with Spanish as our language, and we will secede from the United States. The whole Southwest could become another Vietnam. Mark my words."[24]

Given the historical precedent of Marxist regimes exporting their revolutions to their neighbors, one can't dismiss such Chicano utterances as the ravings of some fringe group. A Marxist Mexico would pose a significant danger to the U.S. and one made even more volatile by the on-going breakup or "Balkanization" process in the United States.

The danger would be of such magnitude that it would take considerable attention and effort by the United States in order to cope. We would, in effect, be abandoning the rest of the world to their fate while we attempt the business of restoring and keeping our own house in order.

The weakened U.S. presence abroad caused by the troop withdrawals will be an open invitation to the Soviets to increase their subversion and adventurism throughout the world. The Soviets would be in a position to seize our oil supplies in the Mid-East and extend their rule over Southern Africa to choke-off our supplies of strategic minerals causing serious consequences to the U.S. economy.

Communism and refugees are facts of life in Latin America. To accept compromise, to negotiate, to appease, or simply to ignore these facts will not lessen the Communist drive for victory over the United States. A victory by simple subversion not by atomic destruction, a victory that can be avoided, but will it?

A ray of hope is on the horizon. pro-U.S., anti-communist, anti-Sandinista Nicaraguan exile groups are operating out of Honduras and Costa Rica against the Nicaraguan government. At this time their effect has yet to be seen.

Surinam and Guyana are two tiny, but useful cogs in the Soviet's strategic plan for the Caribbean.

In February, 1980, tiny pro-Western Surinam (formerly Dutch Guyana), was seized by a left wing military strongman Lt. Col. Desi Bouterse, who has been moving the country into the Soviet/Cuban camp ever since. In December, 1982, Bouterse executed his entire 15 man political opposition, and, in spite of booting the Cubans out at the end of 1983, Surinam can still be considered a Soviet foothold in South America. This is a dubious distinction it holds with Guyana.[25]

Surinam's 300,000 population is made up mainly of Creoles, Hindustanis, Indonesians, Chinese and other small indigenous groups.

The U.S. built airfield at Paramaribo can be expanded and improved to handle Soviet aircraft. This will provide support and reinforcing capability to Cuba, Guyana and Grenada when the islands of the lesser Antilles are targeted to Cuba's newly formed amphibious force. It may also serve as a staging base for the newly declared "Amazonia People's Republic" that the communists are trying to carve out of southern Columbia, Venezuela and Northern Brazil.

Guyana has recently received substantial military aid from Cuba to aid in its border dispute with Venezuela. There is still a shroud of secrecy over as many as ten military airfields under construction in the remote northwestern part of that country.[26]

Secret or not, there is little question but that these facilities will be used to attack U.S. interests in this Hemisphere.

Notes

1. Lewis A. Tambs, "Guatemala, Central America And The Caribbean." Congressional Record, Vol. 128, 25 Feb. 1981, p. 1211.
2. "The Threat Posed by Soviet Expansionism" White House Digest, July 6, 1983, p. 6.
3. Lewis A. Tambs, "Crisis In The Caribbean: A Glance Ahead." Congressional Record Dec 13, 1979, S. 18432-33.
4. "The Threat" White House Digest p. 6.
5. R. Bruce McColm "Central American And The Caribbean: The Larger Scenario." Strategic Review, Summer 1983, p. 33.
6. "The Soviet/Cuban Threat and Build Up In The Caribbean" White House Digest, July 6, 1983, p. 2.
7. "The Military Balance 1983/84" (Cuba), Air Force Magazine December 1983, p. 122-123.
8. Tambs, "Crisis In The Caribbean," p. S. 18432-33.

9. Background Paper: Central America, State Department and The Department of Defense, May 27, 1983, p. 3.
10. Donald S. McAlvany, "Revolution In Central America," The McAlvany Intelligence Advisor, May, 1983, p. 5-6.
11. "Spreading Soviet/Cuban Intervention Throughout The Region," White House Digest, July 13, 1983, p. 3.
12. Ibid. p. 3.
13. Ibid. p. 5.
14. Fred C. Ikle, "Soviet Imperialism Spreads South." Defense. March 1982, p. 26.
15. "The Military Balance," Air Force, p. 124.
16. McAlvany, "Revolution In Central America," p. 7.
17. Ibid, p. 7.
18. Ibid, p. 7.
19. Ibid, p. 8.
20. Ibid, p. 9.
21. Ronald Yates, "Chicano Plan: "Give Southwest Back To Mexico," Chicago Tribune, December 21, 1980, p. 18 sec. C.
22. Ibid.
23. Ibid.
24. Ibid.
25. John Rees "The Communist Effort To Grab Control Of Central America To Threaten The U.S." Review of the News 10 August 1983, p. 34-35.
26. Ibid, p. 34-35.

World Choke Points

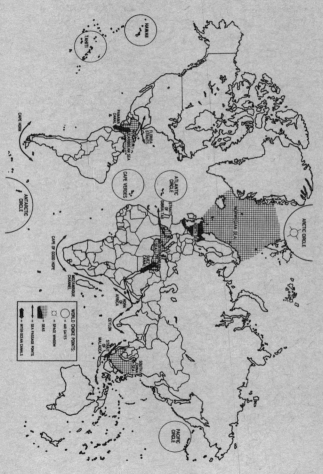

by Dana Lombardy, with the assistance
of Darf McIoyni and Frank Speyers

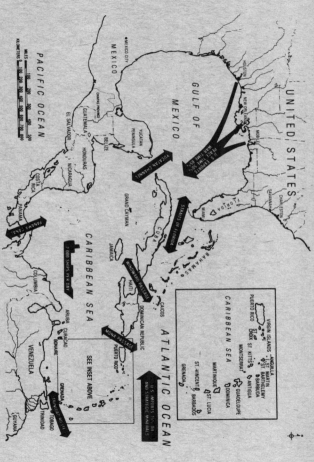

Trade Routes to Gulf Ports

by Dana Lomberg, with the assistance of Duf McLoyd and Frank Speyers

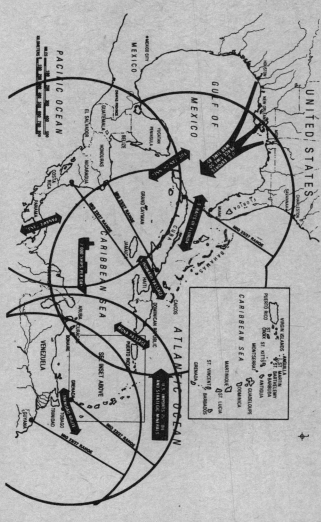

Soviet MIG Fighter-Bomber Ranges Showing
Ability to Cut Trade Routes to Gulf Ports

by Dana Lombardy, with the assistance
of Darf McJoynt and Frank Speyrs

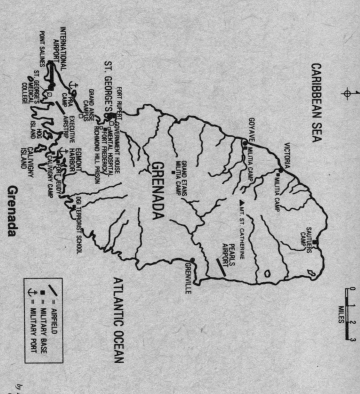

Grenada

CARIBBEAN SEA

GRENADA

ATLANTIC OCEAN

POINT SALINES
INTERNATIONAL AIRPORT

ST. GEORGE'S MEDICAL COLLEGE

FRA CAMP

ST. GEORGE'S

FORT RUPERT
GOVERNMENT HOUSE
MENTAL HOSPITAL
FORT FREDERICK
RICHMOND HILL PRISON

GRAND ANSE CAMPUS

EXECUTIVE AIRSTRIP

HOG ISLAND

FORT LUCAS
EGMONT HARBOR

CALIVIGNY CAMP

CALIVIGNY ISLAND

DGI TERRORIST SCHOOL

GOYAVE MILITIA CAMP

VICTORIA

GRAND ETANS MILITIA CAMP

MILITIA CAMP

▲ MT. ST. CATHERINE

SAUTEURS CAMP

PEARLS AIRPORT

GRENVILLE

N

0 1 2 3
MILES

╱ = AIRFIELD
■ = MILITARY BASE
⚓ = MILITARY PORT

by Dana Lombardy, with the assistance of Duff McJoynt and Frank Spyers

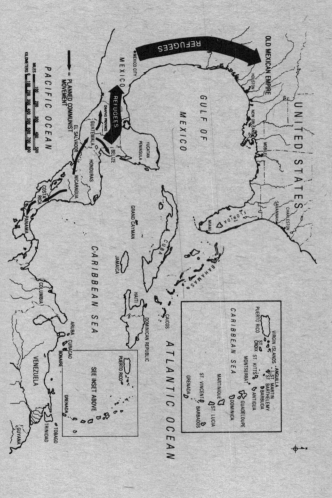

Planned communist movements through Mexico into South West
United States if all goes according to Soviet designs in Central America

by Dana Lombardy, with the assistance
of Darf McIoynt and Frank Speyers

4

THE UNITED STATES
AND THE CARIBBEAN REGION

To understand the significance of the Grenada action, one must realize the strategic importance of the Caribbean region. Grenada is a small tiny island in the Caribbean. Its strategic value, however, far outweights its size.

To appreciate its value it is first necessary to examine it as a part of the whole Caribbean basin, which is extremely important to the national security of the United States.

The United States' southern flank is bounded by two areas—the Gulf of Mexico and the Caribbean Basin. The Gulf of Mexico is bounded on the west by Mexico; to the north by the states of Texas, Louisiana, Mississippi, Alabama and to the east by the state of Florida. It ends with the Bahama, Turks and Caicos Islands.

Acting as barriers to the south between the Gulf of Mexico and the Caribbean Seas lies Cuba, Hispanola, Jamacia and Puerto Rico. These islands also divide North from South America.

The western portion of the Caribbean Basin is bounded by the Yuctan Peninsula of Mexico, the Central American countries — Belize, Honduras, El Salvador, Nicaragua, Costa Rica and Panama. To the south lie the South American countries — Columbia, Venezuela, Guyana and Surinam — front the Atlantic Ocean. The geographical proximity of Guyana and Surinam profoundly effects the region and makes their inclusion necessary.

At the border of Venezuela and Guyana an outer rim of islands arc north toward Puerto Rico to include Trinidad, Tobago, Barbados Islands, and the windward, leeward, Virgin island groups of the lesser antilles.

The Gulf ports were originally built by colonial France and Spain. They took advantage of the marvelous system of rivers that services the interior two-thirds of the continental United States. The largest system is the Mississippi-Ohio River basin. Today, as they have for centuries, these river systems provide a highly economical method of moving goods in bulk from the industrial and agricultural heartlands to an ocean port.

A stable and friendly group of countries in the Caribbean Region are vital to the safety of the United States and to the Western hemisphere as a whole. A glance at a map will show that not only could it be termed part of our southern border, but the area is of crucial concern to our survival.

By virtue of its sovereignty over Puerto Rico, U.S. Virgin Islands, and over a dozen islands, the United States is a Caribbean nation.[1] It is an area where a host of vital U.S. interests intersect. Among these are the stable, friendly, neighbors, trouble-free national borders and, of critical importance, unhampered access to the vital sealanes that flow into the Caribbean Sea.

If this area should ever be dominated by regimes hostile to us, or if it becomes the scene of prolonged social upheavals, the impact on our own society's economy and security would, indeed, be very ominous.

"History passes, but geography remains"[2] is a basic theme of geopolitics. The closed seas of the Caribbean Region have been the scene of strife since the emergence of Modern Europe. All the great maritime nations — Spain, the Netherlands, Great Britain, the United States and the Soviet Union — at one time or another have strived for supremacy.

The early American statesman Henry Clay appreciated the importance of Cuba as well as Puerto Rico. In a letter which he wrote to Mr. Middleton, U.S. Minister to Russia, on the 26th of December, 1825, Clay directed Middleton to inform the Russian Government that "We cannot allow the transfer of these islands to any European power."[3]

He was even more emphatic in a dispatch to the American Minister in Paris, with instructions to pass on to the French Government, "that we should not consent to the occupation of these islands by any other European power than Spain, under any circumstances what so ever."[4]

Any further weakening of the U.S. position in the region's two closed seas — Gulf of Mexico and the

Caribbean—would significantly bring about the collapse of America as a global power.

An advesary bringing revolution to the southern border of the United States would cause the U.S. to pull its forces back from Western Europe and Asia to defend the national boundaries of the United States. Western Europe, Southeast Asia, and the Western Pacific would then be exposed to the full military and political leverage of the Eastern Bloc.[5]

The United States relys on foreign sources for over half of the thirty-two minerals essential for industrial and military use. It also imports over one third of its oil.

The primary thrust of long-term Soviet strategic objectives in the region seems equally clear. Create, through a Soviet naval and air presence and enhanced Cuban forces, an offensive interdiction capability effective enough to block, and thus deny, the U.S. the economically important sea lanes. Another effect would be the disruption of the Pacific-Atlantic military seaborne movements of forces moving to or from the region.

The Straits of Florida, north of Cuba, constitutes the only direct sea lane between the Gulf of Mexico and the Atlantic Ocean. Three channels cut through the Greater Antilles to connect the two American continents. Of those, the Yucatan Channel lies west of Cuba, and is the only direct sea lane between the Gulf of Mexico and the Caribbean Sea.

There are two other channels which provide access between the Caribbean Sea and the Atlantic Ocean. The Windward Passage lies east of Cuba and the Mona Passage passes between the Dominican Republic and Puerto Rico. The lesser Atlantic approaches, including the Trinidad route, lie scattered along the Caribbean's leeward and windward islands.

The only direct access to the Pacific Ocean from the Caribbean Sea transects the Isthmus of Panama and is one of two interoceanic canals in the world. The Panama Canal saves a 8,000 mile journey around Cape Horn.

Strategically, the Gulf of Mexico is more vital to our economic and military interests than even the Persian Gulf. The Gulf ports of Houston, Galveston, Beaumont, Mobile and New Orleans handle fifty percent of the U.S. exports and seventy-five percent of the oil and strategic materials imports. During the pre-nuclear area most of our largest military installations and military equipment manufacturing and storage depots were located west of the Appalachian Mountains. They were located here because of strategic depth and their rapid availability via river transportation to the Gulf ports. According to Navy Secretary John Lehman, eighty-five percent of the military logistics must move from these ports in the event of wartime contingency.[6]

Control of the Caribbean chokepoints particularly the Straits of Florida, Yucatan Channel, Mona Passage and the Panama Canal is the difference between winning and losing a major war almost anywhere in the world where U.S. forces would be required.

U.S. military response must place great emphasis on the use of the Gulf ports and access to the

Caribbean channels. Why, because the east coast ports could handle the output of equipment only to the extent that it could get across the Appalachian Mountains to those ports. There would be a significant delay, and every day's delay compounds our problem in the effort to support our troops and allies, especially in Europe. With the Soviet short war scenario, we can't afford any more delay than is necessary.

The Germans didn't overlook the Caribbean in World War II. Their submarines infested the Straits of Florida and destroyed large amounts of tonnage moving through the vital chokepoints. From January to August 1942, over 260 Allied merchant ships totaling 1½ million tons were sunk by German submarines in the region between Florida and the entrance to the Panama Canal. Forty-one merchant ships were sunk in the Gulf of Mexico in May alone. Almost half the ships lost were oil tankers. In all of those months there were never more than 12 and usually around eight U-boats operating in American waters to the west and south of Cuba. Those submarines were operating four thousand miles away from their bases on the coast of France. They were outside the range of the German airforce and had no support from the German surface fleet. There were no long-range aircraft to help direct the U-boats to fruitful targets or to defend them against attacks by Allied escort ships and patrol planes. When the subs had fired all their torpedos and were running short of fuel, they had to return back across the Atlantic to their bases in the Bay of Biscay.[7]

Soviet planners and theoreticians are not geographic and historical illiterates. They have studied "the Great Patriotic War" and can read a map. Admiral S. G. Gorshkov in his book *The Sea Power of the State* speaks often on the significance of the Caribbean Region:

"The main transoceanic cargo flows in the North Atlantic pass in directions linking the ports of Western Europe to the ports of North America; . . . and the ports of Western Europe with the ports of Central and South America and the countries of the Pacific through the Panama Canal . . ."[8]

The Panama Canal, although termed obsolete by some defense planners, during the Korean and Vietnam conflicts was the key funnel for troops and materials. The canal currently remains the wrench pin for the three ocean presence—Atlantic, Pacific and Indian Oceans—of the U.S. Navy. Only 13 ships in the U.S. Navy, all aircraft carriers, are too large to make the transit.

Hostile Naval and air forces operating from protected bases in Cuba, Nicaragua, Grenada, Surinam and Guyana with modern Soviet equipment are a significant dangerous threat. These forces could effectively deny U.S. seaborne reinforcements and resupply by closing the major chokepoints including the Panama Canal in the region's sea lanes.

Of equal importance, these forces can strike within minutes the major sea ports from New Orleans to Savannah, Georgia, with high performance MIG 23/27 aircraft. The BEAR and BACK-FIRE bombers can also strike or launch cruise missles on remaining ports from San Diego to New York and directly threaten the mid-Atlantic sea routes.

Maritime trade is the economic lifeline for most of the nations in the area. Two thousand ships pass daily through these waterways. Over 1.1 billion tons of shipping representing 68 billion dollars pass through the Caribbean annually.[9] Of this volume, nearly half is intended for, or originates from, the Gulf Coast of the United States. Twelve percent of all U.S. trade is with the Latin American market. Seventy-five percent of all oil imported into the U.S. transits the Caribbean. The Caribbean rim and basin is a petroleum focal point. Through Caribbean channels, Antillean passages and the Panama Canal comes the petroleum of the Middle East, South America and Alaska. The Middle East may be the petroleum pump, but the Caribbean is the nozzle. Super tankers sailing from the Persian Gulf around the cape of Africa do not dock directly in the U.S. Atlantic or Gulf ports. These huge vessels transfer their cargo at the Bahamas, the Virgin Islands, Trinidad, or Curacao-Aruba into standard size tankers which then sail on to the eastern or southern seaboards of the United States.[10]

Venezeulan oil also moves northward through the Mona, Windward and Yucatan Channels. Not all of this oil is crude. Since the U.S. has not completed a new refinery in years much of this imported petroleum is finished product having been processed at off shore locations.

The Panama Canal also plays an important role in U.S. energy supply. Oil from Alaska and Ecuador passes through the Pacific-Atlantic pipeline in the Republic of Panama. This augments the tanker routes through the Canal. Another trans-isthmian conduit under construction for Alaskan oil runs across Guatemala from the Pacific coast to the Gulf of Honduras.

Oil transportation is not the only question that dominates the oil importance of the Caribbean region. Caribbean region nations of Mexico, Venezuela and Guatemala are large oil producers in their own right. They currently provide the U.S. with thirty percent of its petroleum imports. Mexico has some sixty-seven billion barrels of proven petro-leum reserves. It could readily supply thirty percent of the U.S. import requirement. Guatemala, which started exporting oil in April, 1981 from the El Peten and West Chancha fields has an estimated reserve of six billion barrels.[11]

The Caribbean region is also a principle U.S. source of strategic mineral imports. Mexico supplies a wealth of materials such as zinc, gypsum, mercury, barium, rhenium, antimony, bismuth, selenium, lead and silver. Guatemala began shipping nickel in 1978 from its sixty million ton reserve near El Estor on Lake Izabel. Nearly fifty percent of U.S. bauxite imports necessary for aluminum production comes from Jamaica.[12]

In addition to these strategic minerals, U.S. steel mills also import significant amounts of iron ore from Venezuela and Brazil. Most of this ore transits the Caribbean. The United States as a mineral and energy dependent nation needs secure supplies. The availability of these mineral imports represents an important economic convenience for the United States today. In the event of a global conflict, their availability would be absolutely essential. Thus, whoever controls the Caribbean Region and its sea lanes could strangle the United States economy by choking off the petroleum and mineral ore life lines.

It is possible for hostile forces in Cuba, Nicaragua, Grenada, Surinam and Guyana to militarily cut off our imports and exports and severely curtail our military war time response.

The tiny island of Grenada is strategically placed in the heart of one of the richest oil-producing regions in the Western Hemisphere. Within a five-hundred-mile radius of the island are oilfields and refineries which currently supply 56 percent of the oil consumed on the eastern seaboard of the United States. They include Venezuela, Netherlands Antilles, Trinidad, St. Lucia, U.S. Virgin Islands and Puerto Rico.

Air and naval bases in Cuba, over a thousand miles from Grenada, are beyond the range necessary for effective offensive operations in the southeastern Caribbean. In the event of war, as pointed out before, this region would be of vital strategic importance to the United States. The destruction of refineries and transshipment terminals coupled with the severing of tanker lanes could cause rapid economic and social chaos. Granada's location allows the giant Amerada Hess refinery and oil storage complexes in

St. Croix (U.S. Virgin Islands), and St. Lucia, to be taken out by MIG 23/27 tactical aircraft in less than 20 minutes.[13]

American and Venezuelan fighters would have ample time to intercept Cuba-based raiders before they could reach their targets. But aircraft from Grenada provides the perfect solution for surprise.

Apart from Grenada's proximity to the oilfields and refineries of the southern Caribbean, the island is an invaluable staging post on the air route to southern Africa. It would also expand the radius of operation of all Soviet and Cuban aircraft in the region, allowing them to fly 1,000 miles into the heartland of South America.

Egmont Harbour, on Grenada is one of the finest protected anchorages in the Southern Caribbean. it provides a superb small naval base protected by the nearly encompassing hills from both offshore surveillance and attack.

Approximately thirty Soviet-built OSA and KOMAR-class missile patrol boats, with a top speed of 40 knots, are now stationed in Cuba. Armed with Styx (SS-N-2) surface-to-surface missiles,[14] such craft would be a lethal threat to the ponderous oil tankers plying the sea lanes around Grenada. Egmont Harbour, which measure 1,200 by 1,800 feet and has a minimum depth of 21 feet, could accomodate an entire flotilla of Cuban missile boats.

Grenada lies at the mouth of the deep trench between the Atlantic Ocean and the Caribbean. This gives it importance for submarine maneuvering. It is for this reason that new submarine-like facilities

found under construction around the deep inlet at
Caligny, six miles east of Port Saline. This inlet is
suitable for submarine operations in the deep waters
that surround Grenada.[15]

In March 1983, in Palm Beach, Florida, Frank
Aker presented a closed brief on the Caribbean
situation. Participants included American conservative leaders in government, business and religion.

Aker's concluding remarks were that Grenada's
strategic importance in the Caribbean is way out of
proportion to its size. A hostile foe there is a clear
danger to the security of the United States and the
rest of Latin America. The seed for action had been
planted.

Notes

1. United States Senate hearing before the Committee on
   Foreign Relations, United Sates Senate, 95th Congress
   on 15 August 1978. Additional protocal I to the treaty
   for prohibition of nuclear weapons in Latin America,
   p. 40.
2. Frank Aker, "Geopolitics of WW III in Central America and the Caribbean" U.S. Army War College.
   Military Policy Symposium 21-22 Nov. 82, p. 1.
3. Senator Cass, "Colonization in North America." Ap-
   pendix to the Congressional Globe, 32rd Congress, 25
   Jan. 1853, p. 124.
4. Ibid.
5. Ronald Yates "The Chicano Plan" Chicago Tribune, 21
   Dec. 80, Sec. 3. p. 18.
6. "In Focus," Air Force Magazine, May 1982, p. 26.
7. R. Bruce McColm, "Central America and the Caribbean: The Larger Scenario" Strategic Review, Summer
   1983, p. 29.

8. Admiral S. G. Gorshkov, "The Sea Power of the State," (New York, Pergamon Press, 1979) p. 12.
9. Frank Aker "Geopolitics of WWIII," p. 2.
10. "The Caribbean" Intelligence Digest, 18 June 1980, p. 1-2.
11. Lewis A. Tambs, "Guatemala, Central America and the Caribbean," Congressional Record, Vol. 128, 25 February 1981, p. 1211.
12. Margaret Daley Hayes, "United States Security Interests in Central America in Global Perspective," Central America: International Dimensions of the Crisis, Ed. by Richard E. Frinberg (New York, Holmes & Meiers, 1982), p. 91.
13. Quarterly Review of Oil In Latin America and the Caribbean, The Economist Intelligence. . . . Ltd. London, 1-3 quarter, 1980.
14. "The Military Balance 1983/84" (Cuba), Air Force Magazine, December 1983, p. 122-123.
15. Conservative Manifesto, No. 31, July 1983, p. 17.

American students at St. Georges Medical School on Grenada surround an American soldier after his arrival at the campus with U.S.-Caribbean forces

Some of the approximately 6 million rounds of
7.62 mm ammunition found on Grenada

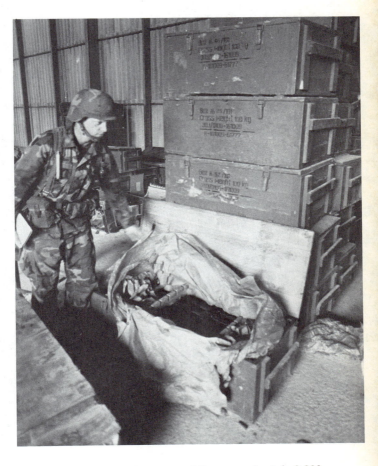

**Crates containing some of the approximately 9,300
individual infantry weapons found in storage on Grenada**

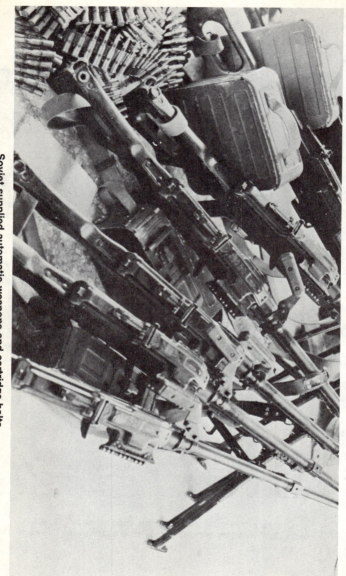

Soviet supplied automatic weapons and cartridge belts

U.S. Rangers display some of the weapons used by the Cuban forces

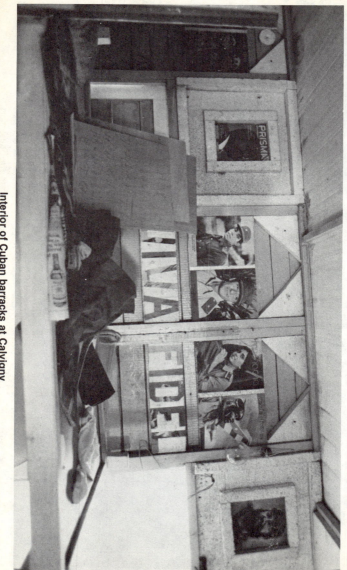

Interior of Cuban barracks at Calvigny

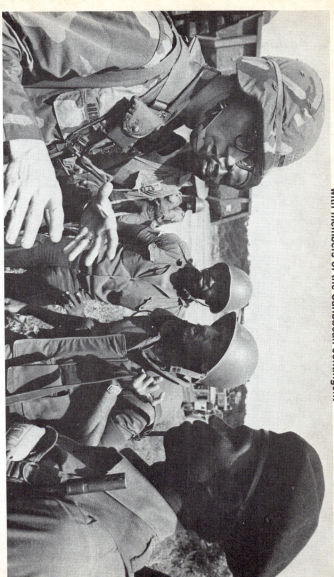

Member of the U.S. team, left, consults
with members of the Caribbean contingent

THE MINISTRY OF DEFENCE, USSR

CERTIFICATE

АН № 46207   _400051_

This is to certify that ....
.... _major_ ....
.... _Einstein T. Louison_ ....
entered in ...._December_.... 19_82_ and graduated
from ....
.... _Vystrel Academy_ ....
.... in ...._May_.... 19_83_
majoring in ....
.... _motorized infantry_ ....
.... _tactical commander_ ....

The bearer of the Present Certificate enjoys
the privilege for independent activity associated
with the Major subject.

Commanding Officer Vystrel Academy
D. Derevsky
"_10_"   _May_   19_83_

Registration No. ___2123___

Military training certificate given by Soviet
defense ministry to Major Einstein T. Louison

5

THE SOVIETIZATION
OF GRENADA

The Marxist interest in Grenada preceded its emergence as an independent nation. Their vehicle was the New JEWEL (Joint Effort for Welfare, Education and Liberation) Movement, a leftist-Marxist oriented political party formed by Maurice Bishop and other middle-class leftists in the early 1970's, most having been educated abroad.

The leaders of NJM made many trips to Havana where they were feted by the communist leaders of Cuba.

Bishop and his pals didn't spend all of their time in Cuba socializing. They took time out to absorb lessons in guerrilla warfare. Guerrilla warfare manuals and Castroite revolutionary literature was confiscated from them upon their return to Grenada.[1]

Bishop's plan, once Grenada got its independence from Great Britain, was to gain power by electoral means and then carry out his social and political reforms. These were, of course, modeled on Castro's Cuba.

Unfortunately for Bishop, a native politician, Sir Eric Gairy, stood in his way.

Gairy was a flamboyant, charismatic politician who proved to be a formidable opponent for Bishop.

On February 7, 1974, Grenada was granted its independence from Great Britain. In the ensuing elections, it was Gairy, not Bishop, who was elected prime Minister of Grenada.

Grenada, under Gairy, was not the model of participatory democracy. But it was a far cry from being a demagogic totalitarian state. The country was moving forward with agriculture production, foreign trade and education.

Grenadian foreign trade, for example, grew from $52.7 million in 1972 to $99.2 million just four years later.[2]

Bishop bided his time and solidified his support with the Castro regime.

By the end of 1978 Gairy had traveled to Chile and had become friendly with Pinochet. This was an unforgivable sin in the eyes of leftists throughout the world. A steady stream of abuse was heaped upon Gairy for this transgression.

Bishop and his movement fanned the fires of discontent by accusing Gairy of not only reaching an accord with Chile, but of cozying up to South Africa. This was a serious charge considering that 98 percent of Grenada's population is either black or mulatto and were in strong opposition to South Africa's "apartheid" policy.

Bishop stepped up his campaign of discreditation against Gairy. It soon became very virulent. So much so that fighting between the two factions resulted. The police resorted to tough, repressive measures.

Gairy, either through ignorance, conceit, or both, failed to perceive the danger to his regime. Bishop had cemented close ties to Castro and had Fidel's decisive support to conduct an uprising against Gairy. It was not long in coming.

The overthrow was carried out with the aid of a team of black Cuban commandos from the Cuban intelligence service (DGI).[3]

Gairy, thinking his situation was secure, was actually in the United States at the time of Bishop's coup, attending meetings of the United Nations.

Gairy showed more sense after the coup as he has not attempted to go back to Grenada and place himself in the clutches of Bishop and his Marxist pals.

For those who still don't think Cuba was involved in Bishop's coup consider: Three days after the coup, the Cuban ship Martanzas showed up in Granada with a cargo of Soviet weapons and ammunition. Now the time required for a voyage from Cuba to Grenada for a freighter similar to the Matanzas would normally be at least seven days.[4] This means the Matanzos was at sea steaming towards Grenada with her cargo of arms at least four days before Bishop's coup. Coincidence—only if one believes in the tooth fairy.

At the same time the cargo of Soviet arms showed up in Grenada, a cadre of Cuban military instructors appeared on the island. A few weeks later, casting aside all efforts of pretense, Grenada admitted it was getting military aid from Cuba.[5]

The Cuban connection solidified in Grenada. Exactly one month after Bishop's coup, Cuba established formal diplomatic relations with Grenada. Named as chargé d' affaires was Julian Torres Rizo. Torres Rizo was a senior official of the DGI, Castro's intelligence service. His speciality was the Americas and he was the former head of the Cuban mission to the United Nations, that cesspool of intrigue serving as a focal point for Cuban and Russian spies in the United States. On October 10, 1979, Torres Rizo was promoted to full ambassador.

In true Marxist fashion, a villa was expropriated and became the headquarters of the huge Cuban diplomatic staff. The villa was heavily guarded and sealed off from the rest of the Grenadian population. No mingling with the masses for these "revolutionaries of the people."

Once ensconced the Cubans began the task of infiltrating the existing ministries of the Grenada government. The Cubans bored so deeply into the affairs of the Grenadian government that the Cuban ambassador became a self-invited fixture at Grenadian cabinet meetings. He often made "suggestion" on policy matters which were seldom challenged by Prime Minister Bishop.[6] Bishop had become a Cuban puppet dancing to the tunes played by his Castroite masters.

Cuba poured military and technical assistance into the tiny island in the months following the Bishop coup. Grenada soldiers dressed in Cuban green army fatigues, toting Russian AK-47 assault rifles strutting around the island, became a common sight. Other Russian equipment such as jeeps, police cars and anti-aircraft artillery ceased being novel occurrances on the island.

An early Christmas present from Fidel Castro was delivered to Prime Minister Bishop on November 18, 1979. It was aid to construct a new "international airport: in Grenada."[7] The airport was being built, according to Grenada officials, to attract big jets bringing in plane loads of tourists. Unfortunately for this scam, there weren't enough hotel rooms on the island to handle the passangers of just a single 747 Jumbo Jet that might be bringing tourists to Grenada. The airport was to be built to serve non-commercial interests — extending Soviet influence in the Caribbean.

The proposed airport, with its 10,000 foot runway, would be a useful stopover for long overwater flights of bombers, reconnaissance and fighters of the Soviet and Cuban airforces. Grenada sits astride the strategic passages entering the inland sea of the Caribbean.

Shortly after the Soviets invaded Afghanistan, Bishop confirmed that his new tourist-inspired "international airport" might be used to ferry Soviet and Cuban forces throughout the region. He specifically shook up the government of Trinidad by declaring: "Suppose there's a war next door in Trinidad, where the forces of Fascism are about to take control, and the Trinidadians need assistance. Why should we oppose anybody passing through Grenada to assist them?"[8]

The airport in Grenada along with those in Cuba, Nicaragua, and Guyana can be used by Soviet and Cuban forces to cut strategic sea lanes in and around the Caribbean.

Three-fourths of all our imported oil comes through the Caribbean. It comes in supertankers around the Cape Horn, through the South Atlantic and passes by Grenada on the way to oil refineries in Curaco and Aruba (These refineries, incidentally are only minutes away from attack by MIG-based planes in Grenada.). Other supertankers deliver the crude oil to the Virgin Island and Puerto Rico where it is refined and then moved by smaller tankers to east and southern Gulf ports. There are nine trans-shipment points within the Caribbean basin to offload oil from supertankers to smaller tankers because the United States has no deep water ports on our entire eastern seaboard which can handle supertankers. This transfer is also done in the Bahamas and Trinidad. Supertankers from Alaska offload oil to smaller tankers which then travel through the Panama Canal and head for U.S. ports.

These ship routes offer tantillizing targets to hostile Soviet and Cuban planes based in Grenada at the new "international airport."

There are also extensive oil production facilities and oil reserves of Venezuela and Mexico located in the Caribbean. The United States, one is reminded, also has extensive off-shore oil facilities, as does Mexico, in the Gulf of Mexico. The destruction of these facilities would deal a devastatingly crippling blow to the United States' economy.

In addition to the oil life lines passing through the Caribbean, the United States relies on foreign sources for over half of thirty-two minerals essential for industrial and military use. Over half of our exports and imports pass through the Caribbean!

All are tempting targets to Soviet forces based in the Caribbean and the airfield to be built by Castro in Grenada would become an important link in the Soviet's strategic plans for the Caribbean.

With Grenada as a Soviet/Cuban base they could easily export their virulent brand of Marxism to other tiny island states in the region. They could easily knock them out overnight by 20 or 30 armed Cuban commanders in a boat — just as Grenada was on March 13, 1979.

The communists didn't wait long to meddle into their neighbors' affairs after seizing power in Grenada.

A few weeks after Bishop's coup, the island of St. Vincent protested an attempt by 16 armed Grenadian soldiers to land on one of its small dependency islands.[9]

In January 1980, Tobago and Trinidad charged that over 200 of its citizens had undergone training in terrorism, guerrilla warfare and sabotage by Cuban instructors based in Grenada. During the proceeding months, a number of Cuban-instigated terrorist incidents occured in Trinidad, which Trinidadians termed "a serious threat to the country."[10]

Trouble-makers from St. Vincent reportedly underwent terrorist training in Grenada in a terrorist school run by the Cuban DGI.[11]

If anyone doubted that Grenada had become a Soviet/Cuban puppet that should have been dispelled by their United Nations vote on the UN resolution calling for the withdrawal of Soviet troops from Afghanistan. Not only did Grenada vote against the resolution, along with Cuba, but Prime Minister Bishop sprang to the defense of the brutal Soviet invasion of Afghanistan. "We certainly support fully the right of Afghanistan to call on any country, including the Soviet Union . . . in circumstances such as these, where external aggression is being faced," Bishop said with a straight face.[12]

This display of ideological fidelity obviously pleased the Soviets. In fact they expressed their pleasure by sending Admiral of the Fleet Sergei Gorskov on a friendship visit to Grenada in March of 1980. The Soviet-Grenada love-feast was now out in the open.

In late May, Deputy Prime Minister Bernard Coard went to Moscow on an official visit. He was wined and dined by the Soviet heirarchy including Boris Ponomorov, Secretary of the Communist Party of the Soviet Union's Central Committee and A. S. Chernyayev, Deputy Chief of the Party Central Committee's International Department.

A treaty, signed by Coard, came out of this meeting. It granted the Soviets landing rights in Grenada for their long-range TU-95 BEAR reconnaissance aircraft. In return Grenada was to receive several million dollars worth of trade credits and machinery, plus scholarships for Grenadian students from the Soviets, Czechoslovakia and Bulgaria.[13]

In 1981 Grenada solidified its ties with the Soviets and its allies. Meanwhile, the Cubans were merrily expanding their military construction projects on the island. Among those were a dirt-strip auxiliary airfield and a small naval facility, which was located in a heavily guarded "national security zone."[14]

Grenadian Minister of National Mobilization Selwyn Strachan told Jamaica's Communist Party that the Soviets and Cubans would, indeed, have access to Grenada's new "international airport."[15]

There is speculation that this speech led to Moscow's invitation to Prime Minister Bishop to visit Russia in July 1982. In Moscow Bishop was welcomed as "chairman of the Politburo of the Central Committee of the New Jewel Party."

At a press conference in Moscow an exhubrient Bishop boasted that Grenada's "strategic aim . . . is to further develop relations with the socialist countries . . . and we want to follow our own way, the way of close relations with the socialist community, the Soviet Union in particular."[16]

While in Moscow, Bishop held meetings with various Soviet officials. After the meetings Bishop proclaimed that he had "concluded substantial economic and political agreements with the Soviet Union to cut his country's dependence on the 'West!' "[17]

Moscow had given him $1.4 million to buy "500 tons of steel, 400 tons of flour and other essential goods." He also got a ten-year credit of $7.7 million to pay for the construction of a satellite earth station. This station, claimed Bishop, was to "give us the opportunity of receiving directly in Grenada all the programs that are taking place on television, on radio and what-not in the Soviet Union."[18]

The Soviet Union also agreed to pay for and

build a new port on Grenada's east coast where Soviet ships would make "recreational calls."[19]

In return for this hand-out the Soviets agreed to buy Grenada's two main crops, nutmeg and cocoa, at Russian stipulated stable prices.

Bishop also said he had signed an inter-party agreement with the Communist Party of the Soviet Union. Russia and Grenada were becoming thicker than thieves.

On the way back to Grenada, Bishop made a stop in Havana to boast to Fidel Castro about his deal with the Soviets. Shortly after this visit Libya gave Grenada $4 million to help build this "international airport."[20]

In September of 1982, the Soviet-Grenada relationship came out of the closet as the Soviet Union established an embassy in Grenada. Named as the new Russian Ambassador was Gennadiy I. Sazhenev.

Sazhenev is a four-star intelligence officer in the GRU (army intelligence). Sazhenev's four-stars indicate that he is a high general in the Soviet armed forces. Now Soviet top generals normally wear three stars. Obviously Sazhenev's extra star means he is something special to the Soviets.

According to the Hoover Institute Russian experts, deputy ministers of defense and foreign affairs wear four stars. Their spot in the heirarchy is between a three-star general and a five-star marshal. Technically, they aren't called generals even though the Pentagon uses the term "Deputy Minister and General of the Army" to describe officers in that slot.[21]

Sazhenev's career in Latin America is part and

parcel of the Soviet Union's active campaign of subversion. In fact, one could almost say, if you find the communists stirring up trouble in Latin America, chances are Sazhenev is somewhere near doing this stirring.

He first surfaced in Latin America in 1961 when he arrived in Havana as a lowly third secretary at their embassy. This was the year, incidentally, the Soviets were putting nuclear missiles into Cuba. Just one year later, Sazhenev had shot up the promotion ladder to become first secretary of the Russian embassy!

In 1969 Suzhenev surfaced in Columbia. His official title was minister-counselor. A minister-counselor, according to Russian experts at the Hoover Institute, is a term commonly used by the Soviets as a means of cover for a military intelligence officer. Most of these officers in foreign embassies specialize in terrorism and guerrilla warfare. During Sazhenev's years in Columbia, from 1969 into the early 1970's, terrorism and guerrilla violence surged in Columbia.

Sazhenev was then promoted to the post of re-opening the long-closed Soviet embassy in Argentina. During his tour guerrilla subversion and terrorism increased in Argentina.

Sazhenev had another skill that looms large in a geopolitical consideration of Grenada. During WWII, he was serving with the Soviet long range bomber force. In addition to his expertise in terrorism, Sazhenev apparently knows a lot about strategic airpower. No doubt, Sazhenev was assigned to Grenada by the Kremlin for the purpose of giving advice on the future use of Grenada's "international airport." Given Sazhenev's background, he doesn't seem to fit the role of an advisor to Grenada's "tourist industry" which was supposed to boom with the construction of the huge airport.

The official blessing of the Bishop regime opened up the floodgates to more aid from Soviet-bloc countries. East Germany sent $1-million worth of modern printing facilities to the government-owned Free West Indian newspaper.[22] They also sent five technicians to show the Grenadians how to operate the new facility. Five East Germans, along with nine Cubans, installed 450 tons of communication gear.[23]

In January of 1983, Cuba gave Grenada a "Sandino housing plant." The plant was not to provide housing for the Grenadians, but to build barracks for the island's military forces. Grenada's armed forces, at the time, numbered a little over 9,000. This is remarkable when you consider Grenada's total population was 110,000.

In March of 1983, a Soviet surveying team visited the island. It was decided that the Soviet Union would build a new port and cement plant on the island of Carriacou, a tiny 11-square mile dependency of Grenada. The site chosen was Tyrrel Bay which had been used by the British fleet in the 18th century.

The Soviet visit just happened to occur while the Cubans were cranking up a construction project to extend the runway at Carriacou's airport. This airport just happened to be within a mile of Tyrrel Bay.

In June of 1983, the Grenada government signed an agreement with the Soviets that would permit the Russians to build a ground communication station on the island. This station was to be part of the

Soviet space satellite system.

It is intriguing to point out that the Soviets signed a similar agreement with the Marxist regime in Nicaragua the day before concluding the Grenada agreement.[24]

In July of 1983 the Soviets sent more military equipment to Grenada. Not all equipment came directly from the Soviet Union as other members of the Soviet Bloc kicked-in their share. For example, included in the shipment were 75 trucks from East Germany.[25]

The equipment, including the trucks and other military vehicles, were kept at a special depot. The conclusion one is led to is that this equipment was part of the Soviet effort to stockpile military equipment in the Caribbean.

As the summer was ending it was clear to all that Grenada was indeed a Soviet satellite.

However, all was not well in Bishop's Marxist paradise. Storm clouds were gathering that would bring events of a far-reaching consequence to the Grenadian situation. Although he wasn't aware of it at the time, Bishop's days were numbered.

Notes

1. Naval Institute Proceedings, December 1983.
2. Washington Report, American Security Council, February 1980.
3. AFP Paris, March 23, 1979. See also "Impact of Cuban-Soviet Ties in the Western Hemisphere," Spring 1980, (Hearings Before the Subcommittee on Inter-American Affairs, U.S. House of Representatives, March 26 to May 14, 1980; pp. 99).
4. Naval Institute Proceedings, December, 1983.

5. Advocate News, Bridgeport, Barbados, May 18, 1979, p. 1; FBIS-Latin America, May 22, 1979.

6. Naval Institute Proceedings, December 1983, p. 30.

7. Free West Indian-Grenada, April 19, 1980, p. 15.

8. "A Minor League Havana?," Newsweek, March 31, 1980, pp. 22-23.

9. Advocate-News, May 18, 1979, p. 1.

10. Trinidad Guardian (Port of Spain, Trinidad) January 9, 1980, p. 1; U.S. FBIS-Latin America, January 14, 1980.

11. Newsweek, March 31, 1980.

12. Advocate-News, January 25, 1980; FBIS-Latin America, January 30, 1980.

13. Havana International Service, June 25, 1980; FBIS-Latin America, June 25, 1980.

14. "War Zone in the Caribbean," The Torchlight, August 12, 1979.

15. Dan Bahning, "U.S. 'Heat' on Grenada: Facts Fuzzy," Miami Herald, March 17, 1983 mp. 1A.

16. Tass (Moscow), July 28, 1982; F17. CANA (Bridgetown), July 28, 1982; F18. Radio Free Grenada, August 5, 1982; FBIS-Latin America, August 9, 1982.

19. Nahning, Miami Herald, March 17, 1983.

20. CANA (Bridgeport) August 5, 1982; FBIS-Latin America, August 9, 1982.

21. Virginia Prewett, "More on Grenada's Soviet four-star," The Washington Times, October 5, 1983.

22. Grenada News, Grenada Information Service, March 1982, p. 3.

23. CANA (Bridgetown), November 17, 1982; FBIS-Latin America, November 23, 1982.

24. Barricuda (Managua) June 14, 1983; FBIS-Latin America, June 23, 1983, p. 6.

25. Free West Indian, July 23, 1983, p. 1.

6

THE RADICALS TAKE OVER—
THE AUSTIN-COARD COUP

Bishop's fall from grace actually started in the fall of 1982. At that time the Bishop regime prohibited the Cuban ambassador from attending Grenadian cabinet meetings. No longer would Torres Rizo's *suggestions* on policy be accepted as the gospel truth.

This act of independence angered the Soviet and Cuban masters and they began looking around for a more tractable alternative to Bishop.

The Soviets and the Cubans became even more livid with anger when Bishop, without any official invitation, went to Washington in an attempt to mend fences with the Reagan administration.

After much hesitation Bishop was granted a meeting with two high ranking administration officials —William Clark, then National Security Advisor to the President, and Deputy Secretary of State Kenneth Dam. They delivered a blunt message to Bishop: if he wanted to become friendlier with the United States, he had better ease his repressive rule and hold free elections![1]

Free elections in Grenada were viewed by the

Soviets and Cubans as akin to the bubonic plague. Now the communists were really alarmed by Bishop's trip to Washington.

Back in Grenada after his Washington trip, Bishop informed his New Jewel Coalition colleagues about his visit to Washington. Deciding to test the United States' sincerity, he spoke of opening a dialog with Washington. He also said he was going to tone down his anti-American diatribes.

The Russians and Cubans were now thoroughly alarmed and decided that Bishop must go.

Cuba encouraged Bishop's deputy, Bernard Coard, to replace Bishop. The ambitious Coard was receptive to the idea. This suited the Cubans and Soviets because Coard was an extremely hard-line Marxist who would become a subservient lackey.

A longstanding conflict between Bishop and Coard erupted during a Grenadian cabinet meeting on October 12th. Coard wanted Bishop to step down because he wasn't moving fast enough to impliment socialist changes in Grenada.

Coard needed firepower to back him if he was going to successfully oust Bishop. He cast around for support and struck paydirt. Army General Hudson Austin was a brutal typical hard-line Marxist zealot who was contemptuous of Bishop's squishy brand of Marxism. He cast his lot with Coard.

On October 13, 1983, Bishop was deposed by a coup led by Coard and Austin. They accused him of the heinious Marxist crime of not being "a true revolutionary."[2] Bishop was placed under house arrest. Austin bluntly told Grenadians that his People's

Revolutionary Army would "tolerate absolutely no manifestations whatsoever of counter revolutions."[3]

It soon became clear who had the real power in the Coard-Austin coup — Austin and his fellow military officers soon emerged as the dominant force in Grenada.

They quickly set up a 16-member ruling "Revolutionary Military Council." This ruling body was composed entirely of officers of the People's Revolutionary Army.

The first decrees issued by the Council banned demonstrations, closed schools, closed down businesses indefinitely and imposed a four-day 24-hour curfew. Hudson bluntly said that any curfew violator "will be shot on sight."[4]

The coup leaders, however, underestimated Bishop's popularity in Grenada. On October 19th a crowd of his supporters, several thousand strong, rushed the residence where Bishop was being held and freed him. To chants of "We get we leader back"[5], Bishop was carried by his supporters to a rally at Fort Rupert in St. Georges to protest his overthrow.

Austin responded brutally as he had threatened. Trucks filled with armed soldiers suddenly converged on the rally. The troops opened up on the crowd, killing about a dozen people. Needless to say, pandemonium ensued as the survivors fled for their lives. In the resulting confusion, Bishop was led away at gunpoint by the army.

Later that night Radio Free Grenada made the announcement that Bishop was dead. He and five others were executed on the direct order of the Soviet Ambassador Gennadiy Sazhenev.[8] Killed along with

Bishop were Foreign minister Unison Whiteman, Education Minister Jacheline Creft, Housing Minister Norris Bain and two union leaders who were close allies of Bishop.

When word of the bloody events in Grenada reached Washington, a naval task force en route to Lebanon with 1,900 Marines was diverted and ordered to head for Grenada. The task force's new mission was to be ready to offer protection, if necessary, for the 1,000 Americans on the island. Most of these were students at the St. George's University Medical School.

Neighboring island states of Grenada were particularly alarmed at the unfolding of the bloody events on their doorstep. The leaders of those nations met at Port-of-Spain, Trinidad, on October 21, 1983 to consider action to protect themselves against the new tyrants in Grenada.

"The worst has been realized," said Barbados Prime Minister Tom Adams. "The most vicious type of political murder has come into what was once a happy chain of islands." The leaders of the island nations each expressed the fear that the bloody events in Grenada would encourage Cuban-supported revolutionaries in their own nations.

On October 20th, Jamaica broke relations with Grenada. Even the socialist opposition leader, Michael Manley repudiated Austin's RMC and cut his party's ties to the New Jewel Movement. Manley also advocated the extreme action of kicking Grenada out of the Socialist International movement!

St. Lucia Prime Minister Sir John Compton said, "Whatever little chance Grenada had in Bishop for the liberalization of the regime is gone for sometime to come. Coard's regime will try to push the Caribbean Community into the communist camp."[7] Compton promised that his government would resist any such efforts to communize the Caribbean Community.

The government of Dominica said it would have no dealings with those who now "unlawfully"[8] constitute the government of Grenada.

"The Government of Monserrat," said its Chief Minister John Osborne, "feels strongly that we (regional leaders) must meet as soon as possible to consider our future relationship with Grenada under its so-called revolutionary council . . . Our sympathy goes out to the people of Grenada."[9]

Even London was shocked by the events. Commonwealth Secretary-General Ramphal issued a statement that expressed horror at the murder of Bishop and his supporters. "I feel sure that Commonwealth Caribbean governments will wish to use every influence through coordinated responses to ensure that the will and interest of the people of Grenada are respected and the integrity of the island-state are preserved," his statement said.[10]

These nations understood that, even collectively, they lacked the power to undo the damage in Grenada alone. They voted unanimously to ask the United States for help. The OECS nations (St. Vincent and Grenadines, St. Lucia, Dominica, Antigua and Barbuba, St. Kitts/Nevis and Monserat) in addition to Jamacia and Barbados voted formally to intervene by force in Grenada if the U.S. would help them.

The intervention would conform to the OECS

charter provision that the heads of government may collectively agree to take whatever measures are necessary to defend the region and preserve the peace.

An urgent cable was sent from Barbados to American Secretary of State George Schultz. It told him the eastern Caribbean states wanted the United States to invade Grenada.

On Sunday, October 23rd, ironically on the same day of the tragic terrorist bombing of the American and French military quarters in Beirut, Lebanon, President Reagan met with the National Security Council in Washington, D.C.

The Beirut bombings convinced Reagan that the U.S. must act decisively in the Caribbean. "We cannot let an act of terrorism determine whether we aid or assist our allies in the region," Reagan said. "If we do that, who will ever trust us again."[11]

At 6 P.M. Reagan signed the order that was to launch the American liberation of Grenada.

Notes

1. Time, November 7, 1983, p. 27.
2. Frank J. Prial, "Army in Grenada Takes Over Power," New York Times, October 17, 1983, pp. 1-6.
3. Ibid.
4. Time, October 31, 1983, p. 78.
5. Time, October 31, 1983, p. 78.
6. NBC Nightly News, October 27, 1983.
7. Grenada: October 25 to November 2, 1983, Department of Defense publication.
8. Ibid.
9. Ibid.
10. Ibid.
11. Time, November 7, 1983, p. 28.

7

THE LIBERATION
OF GRENADA

Reports indicate President Reagan first began thinking about a military intervention in Grenada shortly after the execution of Bishop. A major concern of the administration was that the Coard-Austin regime would hold the American medical students attending St. George's Medical School as hostages.

President Reagan was determined that there would not be a repeat of the Iranian hostage situation in Grenada.

The week before the invasion, Donald Cruz, a U.S. consular official stationed in Barbados flew to Grenada to assess the situation. There he was told by the medical students that they were scared of the situation as a result of the coup by Coard and Austin.

Cruz's report alarmed the administration. Grenada's Governor General Sir Paul Scoon, held in virtual house arrest by the new Grenadian regime, had smuggled a message out to Prime Minister Tom Adams of Barbados. Scoon reported on the chaos sweeping the island and called for help.

Adams consulted with other members of the Eastern Caribbean Island Nations and sent a cable to Washington asking for help in the crisis from the United States.

The Reagan administration was eager to help and the decision was made on Sunday, October 23, 1983 to answer Scoon's plea for help.

The U.S. Amphibious Assault Force had arrived in the area of operations and began the deception plan to draw the island's defenders away from key objectives. Early on Tuesday, October 25, 1983, the United States launched Operation Urgent Fury, the military liberation of Grenada.

The operation opened with a two-pronged assault.

At 5:36 A.M. Marines from the amphibious assault ship Guam disembarked from their helicopters on Pearls airport, Grenada's only functioning airstrip. The Marines encoutered little resistance from the Grenadian army and Cuban defenders and seized control of the airport within two hours.

The second prong of the assault called for Army Rangers to make an airborne assault and secure the unifnished 10,000 foot airstrip at Point Salines on Grenada's southeastern tip.

The original plan was to send in a small element of Rangers via parachute to seize and clear the airstrip while the rest of the Rangers would land and disembark from the C-130 transports. Two hours out from Grenada a change was made in the plan. As much of the force of Rangers as possible would make the jump. Only vehicle drivers and other personnel required to man heavy equipment would remain on the aircraft.

Shortly after dawn the C-130 Hercules aircraft roared across Point Salines and the Rangers jumped at 500 feet, decending towards the surprised Cubans.

Fortunately for the Rangers, the Cubans had anticipated an amphibious assault by Marines. They had placed their guns on surrounding hills facing the sea and, as a result, could not depress them enough to bring effective fire on the Rangers at the airstrip. The Cubans also had deployed much of their force in the wrong place. Only one company of Cuban soldiers was on the airstrip near the tower. Two other companies were on the reverse slope of the hill waiting for the Marine landing that never came.

Nevertheless, the Rangers were facing more than 600 well armed professional soldiers. The Cubans met the soldiers with automatic-rifle fire as the Rangers landed. The Randers took cover and started challenging the defenders with return fire.

One of the reasons for the stiff Cuban resistance could have been the fact they knew the Americans were coming.

According to Edward Seaga, Prime Minister of Jamaica, plans for the invasion of Grenada were leaked to Army leader General Hudson Austin by one of the Caribbean Community (Caricom) countries that took part in the regional summit called to discuss the Coard-Austin coup.

"When at the meeting at the weekend we discussed

the plan for invasion we are fortunate that we never mentioned a time or a date, because when I visited Grenada today I was told that immediately after the meeting was over those plans were given to General Austin in Grenada," Seaga told a rally of his Jamaica Labour Party (JLP) in Jamaica.[1]

Seaga called the leaking of the plans an "everlasting disgrace" of the country involved, which he refused to name.

However, most observers feel strongly that Seaga was referring to leftist Guyana, whose President, Forbes Burnham, was extremely critical of the U.S. action. It was also Guyana who co-sponsored a UN Security Council resolution condemming the U.S. action in Grenada, which the United States vetoed.

Burnham was outspoken in his opposition of the idea of an armed intervention of Grenada at the Caricom summit.

When the Caricom summit failed to reach a consensus on the Grenadian crisis, the Organization of East Caribbean States (OECS), the regional subgroup representing the Leeward and Windward Islands, caucused quietly with Jamaica and Barbados to invite the U.S. to liberate Grenada.

Seaga said that there was concern that there had been any forewarning of the invasion "those vicious butchers"[2] who were at the helm in Grenada would have held Americans on the island hostage and killed the governor-general, Sir Paul Scoon, who was under house arrest in Grenada.

"Hence we made our plans in great secrecy. Hence, we did not express the plans to those countries who are now complaining they didn't know, because we did not want anything to leak out and it is a good thing that we made it in secrecy because we had traitors among us,"[3] Seaga told the October 31st rally.

The reference to countries complaining of having not been told about the plans apparently came from Tobago's George Chambers' statement that he heard nothing more of the intention until after troops had landed on Grenada.

If Seaga's statements are true it would indicate that the Cubans on Grenada knew the Americans were coming but didn't know exactly when or where.

Leading credence to Seaga's credibility is the fact that on October 24th, the day before the American action, Austin's regime presented a note to the United States seeking assurance that the U.S. was not planning an invasion of Grenada.

On the same day, October 24th, the Grenada press reported that the OECS, plus Jamaica and Barbados, were planning to invade Grenada.[4]

The fact that the Americans faced tough resistance from professional soldiers instead of so-called "construction laborers" indicates the Cubans were bracing for an American intervention.

The biggest factor going for the U.S. Rangers facing the stuborn resistence of the Cuban "Construction laborers/professional soldiers" was the availability and use of overwhelming firepower. The Rangers utilized their available weapons to maximum advantage.

A key weapon was the AC-130 Spectre gunships

which reined thousands of bullets down on the resisting forces. One Ranger described the gunships as "just like having a sniper in the sky."[5]

The Cubans had placed boulders, vehicles and pipes on the runway to deny its use to troop landing aircraft. They also drove some spikes into the runway to prevent its use. (If the defenders weren't expecting hostile forces, one should ask: why were they rending the airstrip useless? After all the obstructions, etc. would also prevent Soviet and Cuban aircraft from using the runway. Yet it was strewn with obstacles. Obviously, the defenders were expecting the arrival of somebody not to their liking and had taken steps to see that they wouldn't use the Port Salines runway as a means of arriving.)

One Ranger jumped on a steam roller and drove up and down the runway driving the spikes into the ground. Other soldiers cleared the airstrip of the remaining obstacles.

By 7:15 A.M., about two hours after their initial landing, the Rangers had secured the Point Salines airstrip. Hundreds of Cubans had tossed away their weapons and surrendered bowing to the superior American firepower.

While the Rangers were taking the airfield, the C-130s that had transported them to Grenada returned to Barbados, the jumping-off point for the airborne assault, to refuel. When the airstrip was secured and enough runway cleared of obstacles the planes returned and off-loaded the rest of the equipment. The first plane actually touched down within 1½ hours after the jump by the Rangers.

Due to the unexpected heavy resistance on the island, the Pentagon ordered two battalions of the 82nd Airborne Division, based at Fort Bragg, N.C., sent to the island. They were needed, said Joint Chief of Staff Chairman John Vessey, because "We got a lot more resistance than we expected."[6]

However, the fighting was far from over as more than 400 Cubans, plus an unknown amount of Grenadians continued to harass the Rangers with sniper and mortar fire. More importantly, they had isolated the Grand Anse campus of the St. Georges Medical School from its True Blue campus. There were over 700 American students attending St. Georges and their safety was one of the prime considerations of President Reagan when he decided to send troops into Grenada.

After securing the airfield, the Rangers pushed on towards the True Blue campus. About 8:30, worried students at the campus heard and saw soldiers near one of the dormitories. As the troops approached the school they shouted "We're Americans. You are all right."[7]

Having made contact with the students the soldiers warned the students to stay clear of the windows, gather their belongings and report to a nearby lecture hall. The students were told, "We are the U.S. armed forces and we are here to get you out if you want to go."[8] Needless to say, the students were estatic, relieved that their ordeal was about to end. The students couldn't leave, however, until American forces could clear stuborn resistance of a Cuban stronghold at Frequente. As long as Frequente was in Cuban hands they could threaten with fire the airstrip. Clearing out the Cubans from Frequente was essential before the Americans could use the Point Salines airstrip for resupply of its forces and to evacuate the medical students. Frequente did not fall to the American troops until after sundown.

This added to the ordeal of the students at the True Blue campus. They could only wait and try not to become over-apprehensive as the drama unfolded around them. A party was organized to keep the students occupied and the school even kicked into the attempted festivity by providing bottles of rum for the occasion. However, the party could not overcome the circumstances the students found themselves in and it was far from a roaring success.

Early the next morning the students were evacuated. Grabbing up all the luggage they could carry, they went to the Point Salines airstrip where a C-141 transport was waiting for them. The paratroopers from the 82nd Airborne guarded the students as they boarded the plane as the sound of gunfire could still be heard from the continuing fighting on the island. Finally, the last student was aboard and the plane prepared to take off. As the plane swooped up into the air, the students all let out a whooping shout of joy. The evacuation of the True Blue campus was complete.

There were still at least 200 students trapped at the Grand Anse campus, some four miles to the north. They were almost out of food and were surrounded by Cubans carrying AK-47 automatic rifles. The Cubans had ringed the campus knowing that the Americans would not use their heavy firepower for fear of hitting the students who were close by.

After securing the airfield and capturing the stronghold at Frequente, U.S. troops began pushing north towards the grand Anse campus. They ran into a series of well laid small arms ambushes. From the hills behind Grand Anse the Cubans also directed RPG-7 rocket fire and fire from armored personnel carriers at the advancing Americans. The Americans decided to leapfrog the Cubans and mount a helicopter assault to relieve the Grand Anse campus.

About 4:30 P.M. one of the students looked out the window and saw "something right out of 'Apocalypse Now' "[9] — the advancing heli-borne assault. A line of helicopters was racing towards the beach. They were accompanied by A-6 and A-7 fighters and C-130 Spectre gunships which were strafing and attacking the Cuban positions around the campus. They laid down a devastating curtain of fire which lasted for almost 15 minutes. So concentrated was the fire it completely flatened the nearby Spice Island and Grenada Beach hotels!

Finally, after what seemed like eternity to the trapped students, soldiers and Marines raced to the campus, kicked down doors and announced, "We're friendly forces."

Having made contact with the students, Rangers popped canisters of yellow smoke to guide the evacuating Chinook helicopters. In small groups, guarded by soldiers forming a protective gauntlet around them, the students left the buildings and ran for the helicopters while shots still whizzed around them. One by one the choppers lifted off and ferried the students over to the Point Salines airstrip. There the students were given food and fruit juice, captured from the Cubans, before boarding a C-141 for their flight back home.

In their haste to leave Grand Anse campus, the students were forced to leave behind thousands of dollars worth of personal property, such as cameras, radios, stereos, and personal clothing.

All the medical students were now off the island but the Cuban resistance was not yet ended.

Although the students had been rescued, another important hostage, the Governor-General Sir Paul Scoon, was still held hostage in his home by Cuban forces.

Scoon's rescue was one of the first objectives of the military operation. That job was given to the Navy's elite SEALS Unit. An 11-man SEALS team had parachuted into the governor-general's residence in St. Georges. They rushed the house but were driven back by gunfire from the guards keeping Scoon under house arrest. The SEALS regrouped, attacked again and took charge of Scoon's mansion. Scoon was waiting for them having placed a sign on his lawn saying "It's safe to come in."[10]

Unfortunately, the sign wasn't correct. As the SEALS moved into the residence to get Scoon and his family, three Cuban-manned BTR-60 armored personnel carriers followed right on their heels. Now the SEALS were pinned down along with Scoon and his family. Since the SEALS were on a quick in and out snatch raid, they were lightly armed. They had no weapons, such as disposable anti-tank rockets, to counter the armored vehicles. They were virtually helpless and had to fend for themselves as best they could. They rushed into Scoon's house along with Scoon and his family where they were trapped for the next 21 hours. Before their ultimate rescue, 10 of the 11 men had been wounded.

Help was on its way as half of the Marines who had taken the Pearls Airport were ordered back to the amphibious assault ship Guam. The Guam lifted anchor and sailed around the northern tip of the island and down Grenada's western shore to rescue the SEALS.

250 Marines along with 5 tanks and 13 amphibious vehicles hit the beach at Grand Mal, about a mile north of St. Georges. Once on land the force sped towards the besieged Scoon residence and ran into still opposition from the Cubans. It took 12 hours of hard fighting using M-60 tanks to ambush and capture the Cuban armored vehicles, before the Marines lifted the seige. The SEALS were relieved and Scoon was evacuated to the Guam.

The Marines then joined forces with the Rangers and the paratroopers and advanced on the last two Cuban strongholds, Fort Frederick and Richmond Hill Prison.

The Cubans fought desparately using anti-aircraft guns to menace the American planes covering the advance on Fort Frederick. After taking a pounding from carrier-launched A-7s and C-130

Spectre gunships, Fort Frederick finally fell.

The American forces quickly moved on to the Richmond Hill prison which they found abandoned.

Only isolated pockets of resistance remained on the island. One of these was Calivigny Point, to the east of the Point Salines airstrip. On Thursday October 27th, the Rangers mounted a full-scale assault on Calivigny Point.

Intelligence indicated that it was a major Cuban training base and figured it would be heavily defended. The Rangers intended to use as much firepower and shock as they could muster to knock out the camp.

Prior to the actual assault, A-6 Intruders from the carrier U. S. Independence and AC-130 Spectres would bombard the camp softening it up for the heliborne assault by the Rangers.

As the helicopters circled offshore, a battery of the 82nd Airborne 155-mm howitzers pounded the camp. The choppers swooped in and the Rangers seized the camp.

The Rangers found a lot of intelligence information in the abandoned camp. The camp at one time held as many as 400 Cubans. Rosters of unit personnel, weapons sign-out sheets and pictures of graduation classes were found. These pictures indicated an assortment of troops from several different nations. It was easy to see that the camp had been used to train forces for the subversion of other Central American and Caribbean states.

The camp had an obstacle course, weapons range, air defense site and barracks. Literature found in the camp showed that political indoctrination and combat training were the main ingredients taught there. Sgt. Maj. Voyes of the Rangers 2nd. Battaltion described the camp as "Fort Benning South."[11]

By late Thursday, October 27th, Atlantic Fleet Commander Admiral Wesley McDonald reported "all major military objectives in the island were secured."[12]

Although the next day he changed his assertion somewhat by referring to "scattered pockets of resistance" and "fighting still in progress"[13], for all practical purposes "Operation Urgent Fury," the liberation of Grenada from Marxist dictatorship was over.

Notes

1. Bridgetown, CNA, October 31, 1983; FBIS-Latin America, November 1, 1983.
2. Ibid.
3. Ibid.
4. Grenada: October 25 to November 2, 1982, Department of Defense Publication.
5. Soldier of Fortune, February 1984, p. 61.
6. Time, November 7, 1983, p. 25.
7. Time, November 7, 1983, p. 25.
8. Time, November 7, 1983.
9. Newsweek, November 7, 1983, p. 72.
10. Newsweek, November 7, 1983, p. 75.
11. Soldier of Fortune, February 1984, p. 65.
12. Time, November 7, 1983, p. 25.
13. Time, November 7, 1983, p. 25.

8

AFTERMATH

The successful liberation of Grenada not only restored order and the rule of law to the island, but also sent three very strong signals to the rest of the world:

1. The United States will no longer tolerate its citizens being endangered by being made hostages by extremist regimes. The humiliating memory of the U.S. hostages in Iran was a vivid memory that strongly influenced the decision to go ahead with the U.S. action in Grenada.
2. The United States is ready and willing to respond with help to beseiged nations in its own backyard when requested to do so by peaceful, democratic nations in the region.
3. The Grenada liberation has put the Soviets and Cuba on notice that they no longer have carte blanche to subvert nations in this hemisphere.

Grenada's location, less than 100 miles off the coast of Venezuela, was part of a Soviet triangular base complex, incorporating Cuba, Nicaragua as well as Grenada, which would allow Soviet and/or Cuban forces to project tactical air power over the entire Caribbean basin.[1]

Within the radius of operation of the nuclear capable Soviet MIG 23 ground-attack fighter (500 miles) are oilfields, refineries and tanker lanes. 56 percent of all the oil consumed on our eastern seaboard — over 6 million barrels per day — comes from these sources.

To give an idea of the seriousness of this type of threat, the giant Amerada Hess refinery and oil storage complexes in St. Croix and St. Lucia could be wiped out by MIG 23s in less than 20 minutes after take off from Grenada!

Exxon has a subsidiary refinery on Aruba, in the Netherlands Antilles that can produce 480,000 barrels per day. It is only 35 minutes away from Grenadian based bombers.

Shell oil has a refinery on the island of Curacao with a capacity of 370,000 barrels per day. Also on the island is a one million barrels per day Shell transshipment terminal. These are tempting targets for the Soviets or their surrogates.

The island of Trinidad, 90 miles south of Grenada, is a target of Soviet/Cuban subversion. Trinidad also imports 140,000 barrels of crude oil per day for refining and reexport. Most of this oil comes from Saudi Arabia and ends up in the U.S. market. Trinidad is also an oil producer in its own right. In 1982 it produced 64.6 million barrels of oil from its indigenous wells.

In addition to the oil traveling these sea lanes, other essential goods pass through them enroute to the United States. Over 90% of the U.S. supplies of cobalt, manganese, titanium and chromium come from Caribbean basin countries or from Africa via these routes.[2] Virtually all of the oil supertankers coming from the Persian Gulf as well as ships bringing minerals from exporting countries in southern Africa use these sea lanes.

The Soviets do not need to control these sea-lanes, although Soviet warships such as the "Osa" and "Komar" missile-armed fast attack craft operating from Soviet built seaports in Grenada and Carriacous could interdict this shipping. All the Soviets have to do to disrupt the trade into the Caribbean basis is to be able to threaten the shipping. By being able to operate out of Grenada's airport the Soviets would have the ability to reach far out into the mid-Atlantic and South Atlantic with their long range "Bear" bombers and would put shipping in these areas at their mercy. A glance at the map showing the range for MIG 27 aircraft based in Cuba and Grenada will give one an instant view of the threat posed to our sea lanes by Soviet/Cuban forces located in Grenada.

Grenada would have provided the Soviets with a jumping-off place for guerrilla and other subversive activities direction against Latin America. The abundance of Soviet equipment found on Grenada gives proof that the island was being turned into what President Reagan aptly called "a Soviet-Cuban colony being readied as a major military bastion to export and undermine democracy."[3] The weapons found on Grenada would have been sufficient to equip two Cuban infantry battalions for 30-45 days of combat.

The American liberation of Grenada was a "major setback for Castro . . . ," Otto B. Reich was quoted as saying in The Washington Times.[4] Others feel that it would force Cuba to undertake a sweeping reevaluation of its foreign policy similar to that caused by the death of Che Guevara in 1967.[5]

Che's death may have forced Castro to re-examine his foreign policy in 1967 and the loss of Grenada may be of similar value today. But, a reexamination is a far cry from what is needed for a stable peace in the Caribbean—a radical change in its foreign policy by Cuba vis-à-vis its attitude towards the United States.

Here Castro is between a rock and a hard place. His total dependence on the Soviets to prop up the Cuban economy makes it virtually impossible for him to break free from his Soviet masters.

What is he going to do? Suddenly renounce communism and admit his twenty-five year crusade to export his revolution was a mistake and expect the U.S. to welcome him with open arms? Not likely— his Soviet master would have him either tossed out or executed like his buddy Bishop, faster than one could blink his eyes.

Nor can Castro slowly relax his totalitarian grip on Cuba and seek a re-approachment with the United States. The Soviet KGB completely dominates Castro's intelligence organization and, in essence, runs Cuba. They are well entrenched within the Cuban government and can call on the Russian combat brigade stationed in Cuba for any assistance, much as the Praetorian Guard protected and imprisoned Emperors in ancient Rome. For Castro to attempt to swing out of the Soviet orbit would invite for him the same fate that befell Maurice Bishop in Grenada—overthrow by hard-line Soviet cadres. Fidel Castro doesn't have a short memory and he isn't likely to repeat Bishop's crime of retreating from the goals of Marxism.

This means that, although Castro may lie low and lick his wounds over Grenada, he will bide his time and try again to spread the poison of Marxism at a later time when the U.S. is pre-occupied or when a more pliant Jimmy Carter-type administration is in power in Washington.

Castro didn't change his stripes after 1967, what makes one think he will today? His masters, the Soviets, are stronger today than they were in 1967. They didn't abandon Castro then and they won't today.

This brings us to the crux of the matter—as long as Cuba is in hostile communists hands, the United States faces a serious threat to its survival from its southern flank.

Thomas Jefferson was the first of our founding fathers to recognize the strategic importance of the Caribbean Basin, when he observed that whoever controlled Cuba controlled all shipping bound for, or leaving, New Orleans. During Jefferson's time New Orleans was our major southern shipping port. Today there are others.

Cuba is a hostile communist nation backed up by our sworn enemy the Soviet Union. The Soviet presence in our hemisphere is an established fact. The Soviet navy is now a blue water navy operating regularly in the Caribbean and the South Atlantic from bases in Cuba.

The Soviets are pouring military supplies into Cuba. These are modern effective armaments which give Cuba the objectives of air defense capabilities and also the ability to control sea lanes of communication. The Soviets have also provided Cuba with attack-type naval forces. These include one Koni-class frigate, two Foxtrot attack submarines and 50 torpedo and cruise missile attack boats. Their MIG 23 fighter strength totals three squadrons and an overall combat capability of over 250 MIG fighters. All this equipment surpasses any defense requirements for the island of Cuba. One can only conclude that the equipment is to serve as a means of some future projection of Cuban power in the Caribbean Basin.

What about the Caribbean Basin? The Caribbean, an inland sea, is a lot like the Mediterranean — it can be bottled up by airpower, which can effectively crisscross the strategic sea lanes of communication.

The Caribbean provides the arteries for our survival. Three-fourths of all our imported oil travels through the Caribbean. In addition to our oil lifelines passing through the Caribbean, the United States relies on foreign sources for over half of thirty-two minerals essential for industrial and military use. Over half of our exports and imports flow through the Caribbean.

Even though, for now, the airfield in Grenada is unavailable to Soviet/Cuban forces, we have airfields in Cuba, those in Nicaragua and Guyana available to Soviet/Cuban forces. Planes operating from these can still wreck havoc on the sealanes in the Caribbean Basin.

So what, you say. Cuba is puny and we can knock it over with ease. It isn't quite that simple.

Let's consider the most possible scenario based on Navy Secretary John Leman's projections and analysis of the Caribbean geopolitical problem, advanced during testimony before the "Kissinger Commission."[6]

"There is heightened political tension in Europe. There are advanced warnings that the Soviet Union might attack across the broad central plains of Europe. (Our plans are predicated on some early warning.) Many years ago we realized it was impossible to station overseas in Europe the necessary forces to adequately confront a Soviet attack with our allies because of financial and political realities. Many Army and Air Force units are "ear-marked" for early deployment to Europe to reinforce our own forces and our allies. Airfields, cantoments are waiting and ready. Forward deployed logistical requirements ease support needs for the first combat missions.

"Tactical Fighter Wings including our most modern F-15, F-16 and older but reliable F-4 Phantoms are located in our southern states. These wings have virtually automatic deployment orders to reinforce Europe. These assets belong to Tactical Air Command with headquarters in Langley Air Force Base. Some fighter wings are located at Langley, Seymour John, North Carolina, Homestead and Elgin AFB, Florida. A rapid decision must be made. Can we afford to deploy these aircraft?

"We have to ask the question. What is the Cuban's role? What is Fidel Castro going to do? If the Soviets move their armor, is Castro going to interdict shipping in the Caribbean? We have many U.S. naval ships requiring transit of the Panama Canal for reinforcement of the Commander-In-Chief, Atlantic. Are Soviet Bear Anti-submarine Warfare aircraft to undertake missions in the Caribbean and off our coasts? The Soviets have submarine overhaul and refueling facilities in Cuba. Will they be operating in the Caribbean? What is the role of the fast, missile carrying hydrofoil ships Castro has?

"Clearly several fighter wings have to forgo deployment to Europe with a new mission to take out Cuba if they start playing a supportive role to Soviet movement in Europe. How much havoc can the Cubans wreck with their fighter aircraft operating across the Caribbean from Cuba, Grenada (Statement made before the U.S. liberation of Grenada. -Ed) and Nicaragua? How much shipping will the Cubans be able to destroy before the Cubans themselves are defeated? What numbers of U.S. Air Force, Navy and Army units will be needed to effectively neutralize Cuba in the event of Soviet advances on the plains of Europe?

"Will Cuba be able to buy with their sacrifices sufficient time for the Soviet Union to seize several thousand square miles of territory? How many days, weeks, will it take the United States to eliminate the threat of Cuba to our vital lifeline through the Caribbean? We don't know the answer, but we do know that the force deployment by the Soviet Union, the arms build up provided to the Cubans, gives them this capability. Even if the Cubans don't move, their threat ties down our forces.[7]

To nullify this enormous threat it is estimated that the U.S. would have to divert over 100,000 men destined for NATO and divert several aircraft carriers for an invasion of Cuba. The time required for an invasion of Cuba and other operations to clear the Caribbean sea lanes is 30 days. The Russians can chew-up a huge chunk of Europe and the Middle East in that amount of time![8]

What, then, is the United States going to do about Cuba? The U.S., most likely, will do what it has done about Cuba in the past—nothing.

Why, one may ask? it is simple—because the United States has waited until its use of force would be an extremely high risk to take.

Over twenty years ago, the U.S. made a half-hearted attempt to use force at the Bay of Pigs. Even that effort was a little too late. To take out Cuba today, a senior military strategist reports, "would be on the order of taking out Okinawa in World War II."[9] That effort in WWII required a half-million men and a naval force of some 1500 ships.[10]

Having the will to win today in Latin America means sticking to a strategic aim of removing the causes of subversion (These have little to do with "social conditions." After all, what terrible "social condition" in West Germany caused the birth of the bloodthirsty Baader-Meinhof terrorist gang?)

This means the United States should respond to Cuban adventurism throughout Latin America like we did in Grenada.

Remember, the Grenadian liberation represents the first time in history that U.S. military power has reversed a Communist putsch and liberated a people from Marxist rule. Think about that for a minute, the only other Communist regimes that have been overthrown since 1917 have been done by other communists. That is nothing more than a falling out of thieves.

The United State's action in Grenada is of historical significance. Marx and Lenin both preached the doctrine of the inevitability of world-wide Marxist rule. Recently Brezhnev proclaimed a doctrine of the irreversibility of Communist rule. Grenada puts those myths to rest. The U.S. military did not only just take an island — they stopped the march of communist history dead in its tracks.

A further string of reverses, such as Grenada, to Cuban adventurism might just convince the Russians that supporting Castro is too much of a drain on their resources. If they ever reach that conclusion they just might pull out of this hemisphere. The only other choice is to physically toss them out — something we won't do.

It is ironic that many of our NATO allies voted to condemn the U.S. action in Grenada in the United Nations, that multi-racial Muppet show. You would think they would have approved the U.S. action that would help clear the lines of resupply to Europe in case of Soviet invasion of their territory. Their short-sightedness is stupid and unforgiveable on their part.

Cuba, then is the joker in the deck for the prospects of a stable hemisphere.

As long as our policymakers choose to ignore this fact, future Grenadas will be an option they must face. Whether they will treat them like Ronald Reagan or Jimmy Carter remains to be seen. It is inevitable that Castro will look for new areas to create mischief—stirring up trouble wherever he can. The problems caused by his meddling won't go away— but they are threatening the survival of the United States today.

Unfortunately, what we'll do about them only the future will show.

Notes

1. Interview with Gen. Wallace H. Nutting, "Attack on the Americas"—American Security Council Foundation, 1982.
2. Statement of Alfred Scheier, Jr. Chairman of the Board of Advance Pressure Coatings Corp. before the Senate Committee on Energy and Natural Resources, June 20, 1983.
3. Grenada: October 25 to November 2, 1983, DOD publication.
4. Grenada rescue called major Cuban loss, The Washington Times, November 29, 1983, p. 6a.

5. Ibid.

6. Briefing for the National Bipartisan Commission on Central America, by Col. Samuel T. Dickens USAF (Ret.), September 22, 1983, pp. 9-11.

7. Ibid.

8. John Lehman, "In Focus" Air Force Magazine May 1982, p. 26.

9. National Review, November 25, 1983, p. 1504.

10. A Special Valor, The U.S. Marines and the Pacific War, Richard Wheeler, Harper & Row, New York, 1983, pp. 410-411.

Appendix A

THE DOCTRINE OF REVOLUTIONARY WAR IN LATIN AMERICA

Background Notes

Spanish Inheritance

1. Spanish culture, temperament and history have proven to be compatible with the *concept and style* of guerrilla warfare (guerrilla means "little war").

2. The first large scale example of rural guerrilla warfare in modern times was conducted by Spaniards in 1808-1813 against the French invaders.

3. Latin America has a very high percentage of young people in its population. There is too little industry in this agricultural area to provide needed employment of excess population and to develop a solid middle class. A potentially explosive situation exists without the stabilizing influence of the U.S. as a dependable trading partner and as a source of productive and profitable investments.

Lenin's Legacy

1. Lenin provided *political application* to guerrilla warfare. he developed a Communistic doctrine of rev-

olutionary war that pits the dissatisfied lower class against the social and government structure that is allegedly abusing it. This has provided many Latin Americans the spark and fuel (excuse) to seize political power by illegitimate and coercive means.

2. Partisan warfare is the only safe, practical means of Communist expansion in this area of the world. It provides the Soviets with a low risk, low cost, low profile approach to the isolation of the U.S. at an extended range from the Russian motherland.

Art and Science of Revolutionary War

1. The Soviets have developed for Latin America an historically and currently successful plan of action for starting, waging and winning a war of National Liberation. This will eventually lead to hegemony of all of Latin America and compromise the U.S.'s ability to be a competing power in world affairs.

2. Moscow and Havana's blueprint (to be outlined) consists of four distinct parts or phases: (a) organization and preparation; (b) limited war of expansion; (c) conventional war and exploitation; (d) exporting and support of contiguous revolution.

PHASE I: Organization and Preparation

(Note: already accomplished in all Meso-American and some South American countries.)

Target Country Selection

1. Underdeveloped countries are Soviet targets of opportunity since they may be in the economic phase of capital formation and, thus, have a few

wealthy families, a small middle class and a large majority of marginal rural laborers. While it was once believed that the existence of a large middle class would preclude a revolutionary situation, the concrete cases of Uruguay and Argentina, especially the former where neither deprivation nor tyranny existed have dispelled this myth. Nevertheless, in Central America where the politics of envy of the *petit bourgeoisie* can be played against the well-to-do producers, the existence of large numbers of unemployed or underemployed agricultural laborers is important. Even in these cases, as Ernesto "Che" Guevara learned to his dismay in Bolivia, other factors such as race and nationalism may prove critical.

2. A choice of terrorist target is a nation which is ruled by one man, party, or single family. *Caudillismo* and *personalismo* combined with *continuismo* facilitate focusing. The charge of corruption is an excellent emotional propaganda tool and the revolution will have an easily identifiable reference point.

3. Most Central American and Caribbean countries have societies which are unable to keep up with the dynamic changes of the world. The society is unable to absorb change allowing for breakdown of norms or traditions leaving a discontent-disoriented youthful population. Youth can easily be manipulated by taking advantage of their inherent impatience and idealism through the use of abstract themes that have broad appeal. These things need not be realistic or attainable, just emotional. Youth are willing to risk all they have, because they do not have much.

Initial Establishment: Stage 1

Leadership

1. Soviet agents have identified known discontent opinion leaders and have sent them for taining in U.S.S.R. for 2-4 years. They have larned how to form and use the political element (infrastructure) to run a revolutionary war. As long as the infrastructure survives-the revolution survives. To this end, numerous candidates are trained.

2. The Soviets have thoroughly analyzed the social class structure identifying grievances as a "cause." The candidates are thoroughly trained to exploit the cause to secure support of factions and people.

3. Soviet emphasis is to develop an indigenous leadership capable of carrying the momentum of Revolution to full term. They must have independent skills to compile an intelligence base needed to formulate campaign plans and to support propaganda objectives and themes.

Back to Homeland

4. Leaders are sent back to their homeland and initially act independently to form their own competitive organizations. Then, as the cream rises to the top, various leaders will merge their organizations to form coalitions under the more successful leader.

5. First major effort is to win over the Catholic Church by whatever means. This is done by supporting the Church, it works with the poor, etc. To win the Church, they win many supporters.

6. Leaders are installed with the concept that this only is the beginning and that their ultimate purpose is to overthrow the U.S. These leaders are committed to a protracted war. They are indoctrinated to fight as long as it takes to win.

Guerrilla Cadres

1. Soviets have identified initial cadre members to be trained by seasoned guerrillas in other Latin American revolutions or in special camps located in Cuba, Costa Rica and Nicaragua. They learn physical conditioning, survival, political ideology and tactics. it is not necessary for the cadre members to be Communist, only that they be dedicated to the overthrow of the U.S.

2. Cadres return to coordinate with the leadership, establish a rural base, to recruit, train, equip and indoctrinate other guerrillas.

3. Individuals of extraordinary ability may rise to positions of leadership within the infrastructure or form their own infrastructure.

4. First actions—to infiltrate members into the policy machinery of mass organizations; news media, unions, schools, cooperatives, Church, armed forces, police and government. They start a systematic destabilzation and misinformation campaign.

Developing Support: Stage 2

1. Bases are established by each faction in inaccessible rural terrain to disperse assets—avoiding a single catastrophic blow. Terrain selected is contiguous with a country's border in or close to a

revolution. Bases in contiguous countries are most valuable in Phase I to avoid government troop encirclement.

Strategic Holdings

2. Strategic holdings in a revolutionary war are not land or space — that is a conventional concept — it is the "hearts and minds of the people." Maps should not show ground held by forces but areas held by people loyal to the revolutionary cause. Rural areas are sparsely populated receiving little direct government protection, assistance and communication. Rural areas will be more susceptible to supporting insurgents if they provide what the government does not.

The guerrilla units dispatch agitators to spread propaganda to immediate area to gain support — provide schools, medical centers, local security, agriculture assistance in return for food, medicine, recruits and information. Hence the close cooperation between insurgents and some international relief agencies.

The concept of dual government (legitimate and revolutionary) emerges.

3. Infiltrated members in urban areas initiate strikes, riots, sabotage, black markets, rumors and agitation of minorities to cause social and administrative disorder.

This initiative will keep government troops and police tied to urban areas. It is cheap to produce, but costly for government to prevent. Best way to purchase time to change attitude.

PHASE II: Limited War of Expansion

Guerrilla Military Activity

1. Basic assumption—a Latin American government cannot sutain a lengthy internal war financially, psychologically or politically.

The guerrillas must keep constant pressure by maintaining the initiative. Key to controlling initiative is knowledge of enemy's position, strength and intentions done by a solid intelligence system set up in Phase I and constantly being expanded to where every civilian can be considered an agent.

Scatter Forces

2. Guerrillas scatter forces throughout the country and initiate disturbances and demoralizing attacks on supply lines, communications such as railroads and bridges. Weak army columns are ambushed. Hit-and-run raids are sudden, vicious and precise execution and rapid dispersal to not allow the government to reinforce, direct air and artillery fires, or isolate insurgents by using paratroops or helicopters. This places a strain upon the government conventional forces by a process of attrition both psychological and physical. Urban activity is stepped up by directly attacking the property and wealth of those in power. Banks are of particular importance both as symbols and as sources of funds.

3. The government, under pressure to maintain world image of stability (politically, militarily and economically), to receive foreign aid, and to have its trade and military alliances honored, will disperse

troops to police the threatened areas. This causes government forces to be weak at all points. The guerrillas can concentrate their forces at the government's weak points, one by one; defeating the regular troops in detail, yet preserving their own strength.

4. Government forces will predictably intensify repression with road blocks, house searches, arrests of the innocent, closing streets. Police terror will become routine along with political repression.

Propaganda

Guerrillas will make excellent propaganda use of this both on a local and worldwide level. To keep the time honored class privileges, the government power will change hands within the family, part, or even be taken over by the military. Government soldiers will begin to show signs of tiring, they will lose faith and decline in morale.

5. Insurgents will avoid direct confrontations while building a well-armed, mobile army, through capture of arms, recruitment and defection of government troops with his expertise.

Terrorism

1. Should for some reason the guerrilla activities fail and/or the government takes steps to remove the cause, then the guerrillas will have no other choice but to seek power by terror and intimidation. This is done by committing atrocities not against the government, but against the people on whose behalf the insurrection is instigated.

It will make no difference to the local or world-wide press — they will still sympathize and call it a guerrilla action in a civil war.

2. Terrorism can never succeed militarily, only psychologically. It is usually given into by appeasement. This is accomplished by propaganda leading to a negative governmental political approach in which it is believed no defense is possible against terrorism. This leads to a nation's moral exhaustion and a predisposition to surrender.

Respond to Terrorism

3. To respond to terrorism an arch-military conservatism develops. This is embodied in a blind adaptation of a European pattern of warfare of ponderous armor and static heavily fortified garrisons. The government leadership is oriented towards war of mobility and clearly formulated objectives of attack, a strategic approach in which armor is the chosen instrument. This will fail against the guerrilla turned terrosit and will result in an increased feeling of defeatism on the part of the military and ultimately fatalism. All the government needed to have done was change tactics and to be prepared for a protracted war. This military conservatism is expensive and will put more strain on the economy than it can stand.

4. Terrorist victory is near when the political element's defeatist attitude infiltrates the military arm. The first sign of this is when the government seeks to negotiate a settlement. This signals the army that the government no longer has confidence in its ability to win.

*Demoralization and Dissatisfaction of the People
with the Government*

1. Extensive propaganda campaigns. The people will judge what is promised by the rebels not what is provided, but the government must run on its record. As more territory is won over and absorbed, enough people will actively commit themselves to the revolution so that "home guards" can be formed. These local vigilante groups are not combat units, they serve as police and protect guerrilla areas. It is their job to discourage loyalists, obtain information, and oblige support and contributions.

Back the Rebels

In many cases, Church officials will back the rebel factions, having been won over by the propaganda that the rebels are dedicated to helping the poor.

2. A long internal war compromises foreign relations: no country or company wishes to invest in a risky area or deal with a toppling government. Many major families will begin leaving the country with their wealth.

3. A long war also causes dissention among the people because the government cannot keep order in guerrilla infested areas. Acts of terror and sabotage occur which make civilians lose confidence in the strength and authority of the government. War weariness and war frustration arises.

4. The government, by constantly increasing the troop strength to confront the guerrillas conventionally, will cause a labor drain and subsequent economic and political dislocation.

PHASE III: Conventional War and Exploitation

Guerrilla Military Activity

1. Equalization of manpower and equipment between insurgents and government troops.

Government troops are overextended and revert to defensive posture around fortified bases in a mistaken belief that they must hold territory.

2. Guerrilla army uses positional warfare to pin and hold regular field forces, while mobile units encircle and then destroy government units. The conventional battles will break the back of the government's army and the will to win will be exhausted.

3. Insurgent's final drive will be to capture the capital. This effectively cuts the head of the government snake and without it the rest will die.

Guerrilla Political Activity

1. Negotiations will be well publicized. The press is particularly fond of this type of media event — real or not. The international media will be used to consolidate and repeat the revolutions's goals, frustrate the government, and influence world public opinion. The only concessions accepted are those that aid the insurgents. (Never negotiate with a Communist).

2. Coalition government — any sign of compromise will be a sign of weakness and appeasement leading to ultimate surrender.

PHASE IV: Exporting and Supporting of Contiguous Revolution

Revolutionary Puppet Government

1. Soviet and Cuban "advisors" will take control of the new government's operations and military. This will leave a rubber stamp government of revolutionary leaders.

2. Internal security will be tightened with any and all opposition brutally disposed of. This organized terror will be coupled with a comprehensive program to direct every aspect of an individual's life — his work and life will be dictated — application of the six principles of retaining power.

Next Target

1. The recently revolutionized country is then obliged to render assistance to all other wars of National Liberation in the area.

2. Citizens of the newly conquered country will be told it is a source of comradeship, revolutionary ideals, and repayment, and that they must provide bases and training camps, troops, arms and ammunition.

3. The best next object will be a contiguous nation — Nicaragua, El Salvador, then Guatemala.

Appendix B

OVERVIEW

THE SITUATION: Responding to an urgent and formal request from the organization of Eastern Caribbean States (OECS), six Caribbean States and the United States joined in a collective action to restore peace and public order in Grenada. Elements of the combined force landed on Grenada early on October 25. The force includes contingents from Jamaica and Barbados plus four OECS member states: Antigua, Dominica, St. Lucia and St. Vincent. The objectives of the collective security force were to restore peace, order and respect for human rights; to evacuate those who wish to leave; and to help the Grenadians re-establish governmental institutions.

COLLAPSE OF GOVERNMENTAL INSTITUTIONS IN GRENADA: On October 19, Grenada's Prime Minister, Maurice Bishop, and several Cabinet members and labor leaders were brutally murdered by a handful of their former military associates. The physical elimination of most of the Government of

Grenada was followed by announcement of a "Revolutionary Military Council" (RMC) and rumors that the remaining government members had been murdered. The only visible act of "authority" was the imposition of a shoot-on-sight curfew.

WHY CARIBBEAN STATES AND U.S. ACTED: The Eastern Caribbean States saw the violence and the disintegration of political institutions in grenada as an unprecedented threat to peace and security of the region. With 800-1,000 U.S. citizens (many, students at the St. George's Medical School) to protect, we shared their concerns. Inaction would have increased the dangers of the crisis in Grenada.

LEGAL AUTHORITY: The OECS acted pursuant to collective security provisions of the 1981 OECS Treaty of Establishment and after receiving a confidential appeal from the Govenor-General of Grenada. The OECS states are not party to the Rio Treaty; the OECS Treaty is their regional equivalent, and is consistent with the purposes and principles of U.N. and OAS Charters. U.S. participation is also justified by the need to protect U.S. nationals. U.S. actions have been consistent with the consultation and reporting provisions of the War Powers Resolution.

CUBAN/SOVIET ROLE: Cuban military units had secretly established fortifications, arms caches, and military communications facilities. Cuban troops were the backbone of resistance to the collective action. Captured documents indicated the USSR and North Korea, as well as Cuba, had made secret treaties with Grenada, calling for the provision of arms and equipment free of charge worth over 37 million dollars.

Taken together, the Soviet and Cuban plans for Grenada amounted to turning this peaceful island from a tourist paradise into what President Reagan aptly called "a Soviet-Cuban colony being readied as a major military bastion to export and undermine democracy."

Appendix C

OUTLINE HISTORY OF GRENADA

- Grenada, formerly a British colony, attained internal self government in 1967. From the 1950s, politics had been dominated by Sir Eric Gairy, whose flamboyant populism and strong-armed tactics were combined with interest in unidentified flying objects and unconventional religion.
- On February 7, 1974, Grenada became independent despite objections from opposition parties, who feared Gairy's inentions, and later accused him of winning the elections of 1976 by fraud. The major opposition party by this time was the New Jewel Movement, formed in 1973 from the merger of two groups and led by Maurice Bishop. It protested economic and social conditions in Grenada and abuses of power of the Gairy regime. Its program stressed socialist and nationalistic ideals.
- The New Jewel movement overthrew the Gairy government in a nearly bloodless coup on March 13, 1979. Bishop became Prime Minister.
- The new government was initially welcomed by

Grenadians and promised to hold early elections and respect basic human rights.

• These promises were never honored. The Bishop regime suspended the country's constitution, refused to call early elections, ridiculed English-style democracy as "Westminster hypocrisy" and turned instead to the Cuban model of "revolutionary democracy," which it tried to implement with Cuban aid.

• Human rights were regularly violated. Habeas corpus was abolished for political detainees. In 1982, there were 95-98 such political prisoners. Freedom of the press and political freedom were abolished.

• Bishop established close ties with the Soviet Union and Cuba. In January 1980 Grenada was the only Latin American country other than Cuba to vote against an U.N. resolution condemning the Soviet infasion of Afghanistan. Five secret treaties with the USSR, Cuba and North Korea were signed.

By 1980, there were approximately 100 Cuban military advisors in Grenada. There were also several hundred "construction workers" ostensibly engaged in helping to build a new airport in the southwestern corner of the island. Much of this construction was military in nature, and many of the "construction workers" has military training.

The October 19, 1983 murder of Bishop and most of his Cabinet was part of a power-struggle resulting from Bishop's reluctance to move more quickly to socialize the economy.

Courtesy of Department of Defense.

Appendix D

CHRONOLOGY OF EVENTS — October 6-24, 1983

October 6-8
- Bishop meets in Cuba with Fidel Castro following a one-week tour of Eastern European capitals in which he sought support for his faltering regime.

October 12
- Longstanding conflict between Bishop and Deputy Bernard Coard erupts in fight in Grenadian cabinet. Coard wants to supplant Bishop and speed up "socialist change."
- Ostensibly as a result of rumor that he seeks Bishop's assassination, Coard resigns.

October 13
- About midnight, Bishop is placed under house arrest.

October 15
- Radio Free Grenada (run by Coard's wife Phyllis) announces arrest of 3 Cabinet ministers. Mobilization Minister Selvyn Strachan announced that Coard had replaced Bishop. An angry crowd of 300

gathered outside the government controlled newspaper to protest. Justice Minister Kendrick Radix arrested for organizing the demonstration.

October 17
• Tim Hector, leader of leftist Antigua Caribbean Liberation Movement, announces that his party is concerned about the safety of Bishop and other leaders of Grenada.

October 18
• Five Cabinet members resign: Jacqueline Creft, Education; Norris Bain, Housing; George Louison, Agriculture; Lyden Rhamdhanny, Tourism; and Unison Whiteman, Foreign Minister.
• Whiteman says that "Comrad Coard, who is now running Grenada, has refused to engage in serious talks to resolve the crisis . . . it became clear to us that they did not want a settlement and seemed determined to use force and provoke violence to achieve their objective."

October 19
• Grenada Airport is closed, flight from Barbados is turned back. Radio Free Grenada, only source of news, goes off the air. Shops are closed. School children demonstrate for Bishop's return to office. Demonstrators force restoration of overseas telephone service which had been cut off. Agriculture Minister Louison is arrested.
• Barbados Government calls emergency cabinet meeting, expresses "deep concern" over events in Grenada.

- A crowd of thousands, apparently led by Whiteman, marches to Bishop's residence and frees him and Education Minister Creft, also held prisoner there. Group proceeds to the downtown area toward Fort Rupert (also Police Headquarters), where Radix was believed imprisoned. Once there, troops loyal to the Central Committee, some in armored personnel carriers, surround Bishop, Whiteman, Creft, Bain and two union leaders, separate them from the crowd and march them into the fort with their hands over their heads. All are killed—Jacqueline Creft reportedly by beating. Wire services (CANA, EFE) from St. Georges report 50 casualties from troops firing on demonstrators.

- Radio Free Grenada announces deaths, formation of a Revolutionary Military Council (RMC) readed by Army Chief General Hudson Austin, and a round-the-clock, shoot on site curfew until October 24 at 6:00 A.M.

- Journalists from international press arrive at airport and are immediately deported.

- Alister Hughes, Agence France Presse and CANA correspondent and director of Grenadian weekly, *Newsletter*, who filed eyewitness report on Fort Rupert events, is picked up at his home by security forces during the night. Hughes was the sole Independent news link between Grenada and the rest of the world. His brother, Leonard, and another businessman, Tony Moore, are also arrested.

- Coard placed under "protective custody."

October 20

- Barbados Prime Minister, Tom Adams, expresses "Horror at these brutal and vicious murders." Describing the new regime he says, "I do not think it will be possible to accommodate so wide a range of governments within the Caribbean. It goes far beyond ideological pluralism. This is the difference between barbarians and human beings."
- Jamaica breaks relations with Grenada. Opposition leader Manley repudiates RMC, cuts relations with the New Jewel Movement and recommends its expulsion from the Socialist International.
- St. Lucia Prime Minister, Sir John Compton, says "Whatever little chance Grenada had in Bishop for the liberalization of the regime is gone for sometime to come. Coard's regime will try to push the Caribbean Community into the communist camp." He said his government and others would resist any such efforts.
- Dominica Prime Minister Eugenia Charles condemns the killings in Grenada; says her government would have no dealings with those who now "unlawfully" constitute the government of Grenada.
- Montserrat Chief Minister John Osborne says events in Grenada had cast a dark shadow over the Caribbean. "The Government of Montserrat feels strongly that we (regional leaders) must meet as soon as possible to consider our future relationship with Grenada under its so-called revolutionary council . . . Our sympathy goes out to the people of Grenada."
- Prime Minister Dr. Kennedy Simmonds of St.

Kitts and Nevis joined other Caribbean Community (Caricom) member states in condemning political violence in Grenada.

• Prime Minister George Chambers of Trinidad and Tobago announced trade and other sanctions against Grenada, describes the killings of Bishop and his ex-ministers as "executions" and said his government viewed with horror the importation of such executions into the English-speaking Caribbean.

• In London, Commonwealth Secretary General Ramphal issues statement expressing horror at murder of Bishop and his supporters. "I feel sure that commonwealth Caribbean governments in particular will wish to use every influence through coordinated responses to ensure that the will and the interest of the people of Grenada are respected and the integrity of the island-state preserved."

• The Caribbean Conference of Churches suspends all relations with Grenada's new military rulers after having earlier offered to mediate between Bishop and Coard factions.

• Emergency meeting of the OECS, plus Jamaica and Barbados, called for Barbados on October 21.

October 21

• Antigua and Barbuda Foreign Minister Lester Bird says events in St. Georges (Grenada) threaten the well-being of the Caribbean. "The Government of Antigua and Barbuda will not recognize the regime in Grenada."

• Except for Grenada, OECS nations (St. Vincent and Grenadines, St. Lucia, Dominica, Antigua and Barbuda, St. Kitts/Nevis, and Montserrat) plus

Barbados and Jamaica formally and unanimously resolve to intervene by force in Grenada if U.S. will assist. Intervention will conform to OECS charter provision that the heads of government may collectively agree to take whatever measures are necessary to defend the region and preserve the peace.

• Grenada's Ambassador to OAS resigns.

• Cuba issues statement asserting its noninvolvement, calls for investigation and "exemplary punishment" of anyone guilty of the Bishop and other deaths, and reaffirms support for the "revolutionary process" in Grenada.

• Curfew lifted for four hours to allow food purchases; riots and looting occur.

October 22

• Caribbean Community (Caricom) heads of government meet in Trinidad; resolve 11-1 to expel Grenada from the organization. Guyana, Trinidad-Tobago and Belize have reservations about military resolution.

• The RMC denies disorder during four-hour lifting of curfew the previous day. On the contrary, the RMC says, people formed orderly queues outside shops, youth were seen playing football, and tourists were at the beach.

• RMC announces "policy statement" on economy, social policy, foreign policy, saying a new cabinet will be appointed "within the next 10 to 14 days."

• RMC announces RMC Lt. Ashley Folkes had been replaced. The RMC states he had been "erroneously named" as a member of the 16-man council the day before.

- The RMC announces Pearl's Airport will be open the next day and that the curfew will be reduced to the hours from 8:00 P.M. to 5:00 A.M.
- RMC issues series of bulletins on Caricom actions, calls for militia mobilization.

October 23
- Fort DeFrance (Martinique) radio reports Grenadian army divided and indicates another coup is possible. Heavy weapons fire is reported.
- Special U.S. Presidential emissary McNeil arrives in Barbados to confer with Caribbean leaders (Adams of Barbados, Seaga of Jamaica, Charles of Dominica).

October 24
- Prime Minister Adams informs Milan Bish, U.S. Ambassador to Barbados, that the Governor-General of Grenada, Paul Scoon, has appealed, in a confidential communication, for OECS action to restore order.
- A charter flight to pick up Canadian citizens is reported unable to land in Grenada.
- The RMC presents a note requesting assurance that the United States does not plan an invasion.
- The Grenadian press reports that the OECS, plus Jamaica and Barbados, is preparing an invasion.

Appendix E

OFFICIAL U.S. STATEMENTS

THE LEGAL BASIS FOR U.S. ACTION IN GRENADA
(From the testimony of Deputy Secretary of State Kenneth Dam before the U.S. Senate Foreign Relations Committee, October 27.)

The collapse of governmental institutions in Grenada began the evening of October 12 with an attempt by Deputy Prime Minister Bernard Coard to force out Prime Minister Maurice Bishop . . .

On October 19 the power struggle exploded into violence. Troops opened fire on Bishop supporters who had freed him from house arrest and accompanied him to Fort Rupert, the Army headquarters. Bishop, several Cabinet members and union leaders were taken away, then brutally executed. Education Minister Jacqueline Creft was reportedly beaten to death. At least 18 deaths were confirmed. Many more were reported, including women and children.

In the wake of these murders, the People's Revolutionary Army announced the dissolution of the government and the formation of a 16-member Revolutionary Military Council (RMC) of which

Army Commander General Hudson Austin was the nominal head.

I say nominal head, because it was never clear that Austin or any coherent group was in fact in charge. The RMC indicated no intention to function as a new government. RMC members indicated only that a new government would be announced to 10 days or two weeks. It cannot be said whether or when some governmental authority would have been instituted.

Former Deputy Prime Minister Coard, who had resigned on October 12, was reported under army protection, whether for his own safety or as a kind of detention was not clear . . .

Against this background, the urgent appeal from the Organization of Eastern Caribbean States (OECS) took on decisive weight. The OECS is a sub-regional body created in 1981 by the Treaty Establishing the Organization of Eastern Caribbean States. Among the pruposes of the Treaty are the promotion of regional cooperation and collective security.

The OECS determined that the collapse of government and disintegration of public order on Grenada posed a threat to the security and stability of the region. The OECS members decided to take necessary measures in response to this threat, in accordance with Article Eight of the OECS Treaty. They sought the assistance of friendly foreign states to participate in a collective security force. Barbados and Jamaica agreed with the OECS assessment of the gravity of the situation, offered to contribute forces to a collective action and joined in urging the United States to participate in the support of this regional measure.

The Governor-General of Grenada made a confidential, direct appeal to the OECS to take action to restore order on the island. As the sole remaining authoritative representative of the government of Grenada, his appeal for action carried exceptional moral and legal weight.

The deteriorating events in Grenada since October 12, taken together, demonstrated the brutality of the RMC and the ominous lack of cohesion within the Grenadian military. The RMC had imposed a 24-hour curfew, warning that violators would be shot on sight, and closed the airport. U.S. citizens were not free to leave. Although the RMC gave assurances that the airport would be opened on October 24 and foreigners allowed to depart, they then failed to fulfill that assurance. It became clear that delay would intensify both the risk of violence against Americans and a vacuum of authority that would imperil Grenada's neighbors.

Collective action in response to the dangerous sitation was consistent with the United Nations and Organization of American States (OAS) charters. Both charter expressly recognize the competence of regional security bodies in ensuring peace and stability. The OECS states are not parties to the Rio Treaty, and the OECS Treaty, which concerns itself in part with matters of collective security, is their regional security arrangement.

Article 22 of the OAS Charter states that

measures taken pursuant to collective security agreements do not violate the OAS Charter provisions prohibiting intervention and the use of force. Similarly, Article 52 of the United Nations Charter expessly permits regional arrangements for the maintenance of peace and security consistent with the purposes and principles of the United Nations. The actions and objectives of the collective security force, in the circumstances described by the President and Secretary of State, are consistent with those purposes and principles.

The OECS states, in taking lawful collective action, were free to call upon other concerned states, including the United States, for assistance in their effort to maintain the peace and security of the Caribbean. Assistance given in response to their request is itself lawful. Moreover, U.S. cooperation with the collective security force permitted the safe evacuation of endangered U.S. citizens. Such humanitarian action is justified by well-established principles of international law. . . .

The President's orders to the U.S. military forces are to cooperate with the OECS in entering Grenada, to facilitate the departure of all U.S. and foreign nationals who wish to leave, and to help Grenada's neighbors work with the people of Grenada to restore order. U.S. support of the OECS military action will be for these purposes only. . . .

We do not at this point know just what steps the provisional government will take. This is for the Grenadians themselves to determine.

One thing is certain: all governments participating in this collective action will withdraw their forces just as soon as circumstances permit.

The OECS acted pursuant to collective security provisions of the 1981 OECS Treaty of Establishment and after receiving a confidential appeal from the Governor-General of Grenada. The OECS states are not party to the Rio Treaty; the OECS Treaty is their regional equivalent, and is consistent with the purposes and principles of U.N. and OAS Charters. U.S. participation is also justified by the need to protect U.S. nationals. U.S. actions have been consistent with the consultation and reporting provision of the War Powers Resolution.

Appendix F

CAPTURED WEAPONS AND EQUIPMENT FROM GRENADA

Large amounts of Soviet weapons and equipment, supplied by the Soviets through Cuba to Grenada under the Bishop regime (since 1979), were found by the multi-national force. The following is a complete list of those weapons and equipment. To place this weaponry in proper perspective, it is sufficient to equip two Cuban infantry battalions for 30-45 days of combat.

Rifles and Machine Guns

1,626 —	Soviet AK-47 Assault Rifle
1,120 —	Model 52 (Czech)
58 —	Enfield
4,074 —	KS Rifle (SKS)
3 —	MK-3
2 —	Bren Rifle
6 —	M-16
2,432 —	Mosin Nagent (7.62 mm Soviet Rifle)
32 —	M-3A1 Submachine Gun
7 —	Sterling Machine Gun
17 —	Sten Mark 2

180 — Soviet M-1945 Submachine Gun
300 — Miscellaneous Sidearms
31 — .22 Caliber Rifles
300 — Shotguns

Crew Served Weapons

9 — Soviet 7.62 mm PKM Machine Gun
8 — 73 mm SPG-9 Recoilless Gun
12 — ZU-23 mm Anti-Aircraft Gun
1 — DSHQ 12.7 mm Machine Gun
10 — 82 mm Mortar

Ammunition

5,516,600 RDS — 7.62 mm
162 RDS — 73 mm
8,962 RDS — 82 mm Mortar
2,320 RDS — 14.5 mm
29,120 RDS — 12.7
86,332 RDS — 23 mm Anti-Aircraft Gun Ammunition
366 RDS — 57 mm Pocket Propelled Grenades
940 RDS — 75 mm
1200 stocks — Dynamite
24,768 — Flares

Miscellaneous Weapons

6 — RPG 7 (Rocket Propelled Grenade)
46 — RPG 2 (Rocket Propelled Grenade)
8 — Riot Gun Tear Gas
8 — Flare Guns
1,824 — Grenades

Vehicles

2 — Armored Fighting Vehicles

ABOUT THE AUTHORS

Frank Aker is a Lieutenant Commander in the United States Navy. Aker is an expert on Latin American affairs. He has a B.A. and an M.A. from Indiana University and a D.M.D. from the University of Louisville. He also has an M.A. from Webster College. Aker is the author of *Hammer of God: 1973 Yom Kippur War* and *The Inflammatory Reaction*.

Morgan Norval is Publications Director for Gun Owners of America and editor of the Gun Owners Foundation newsletter, *Insight*. Norval is author of *Take My Gun If You Dare*. He is an ex-marine who has written several magazine articles on fighting communist terrorism in Southern Africa.

Gun Owners Foundation
5881 Leesburg Pike
Falls Church, VA 22041

Gentlemen:

I have read *Breaking the Strangle Hold: The Liberation of Grenada* and would like to have more information about the work of Gun Owners Foundation.

I understand that you publish books and have a newsletter and other publications.

Please send me information and put me on your mailing list.

_____
name

_____
address

_____
city, state, zip

☐ I'm enclosing a tax-deductible donation to help
   defray expenses.

Refugee Relief International, Inc.
1105 Balmora Drive
Lafayette, CO 80026

Gentlemen:

I have read *Breaking the Strangle Hold: The Liberation of Grenada*.

I would like to participate in the humanitarian effort to relieve the suffering caused by communist imperialism.

Please send me information about your efforts the aid refugees, particularly in Central America.

_____
name

_____
address

_____
city, state, zip

☐ I'm enclosing a tax-deductible contribution to
   help speed desperately needed medical supplies
   to refugees in Central America who have fled
   communist tyranny.

Remnant Review
P.O. Box 8204
Fort Worth, TX 76112

Gentlemen:

I have read *Breaking the Strangle Hold: The Liberation of Grenada* and would like to have more information about your newsletter which warns its readers about the often dangerous economic policies of the government.

Please send me information describing *Remnant Review*. I want to know more about planning for my future in the face of so much uncertainty.

_____
name

_____
address

_____
city, state, zip

Western Goals
104A South Columbus Street
Alexandria, VA 22314

Gentlemen:

I learned of your organization in *Breaking the Strangle Hold: The Liberation of Grenada*.

I understand that Western Goals was founded by the late Congressman Larry MacDonald and is dedicated to the promotion of pro-Western Civilization values.

Please send me a free brochure describing your published works and audio-visual documentaries on the nature of the communist threat to Western freedom.

_____
name

_____
address

_____
city, state, zip

☐ I'm enclosing a tax-deductible contribution to help defray expenses.

Gun Owners Foundation
5881 Leesburg Pike
Falls Church, VA 22041

Gentlemen:

I want _____ extra copies of *Breaking the Strangle Hold: The Liberation of Grenada*. I understand that the first copy costs $4.95, but that all additional copies (if placed with this order) are only $2.50 each. Enclosed is my check, money order, or cash for $4.95 (plus $_____).

_____
name

_____
address

_____
city, state, zip

Carribean Christian Ministries
United States Office
203 East Camp McDonald Road
Prospect Heights, IL 60070

Dear Sirs:

I heard about your mission from the book *Breaking the Strangle Hold: The Liberation of Grenada.*

I am interested in learning more about your work to apply the Gospel of the Lord Jesus Christ to Communism, Socialism, and Humanism so as to prevent future Grenadas.

Captured documents from Grenada prove that the Church is the greatest threat to Communism. By educating pastors, civil government officials, the media and the masses, it is working to keep Carribean nations from again becoming the puppets of anti-Christian philosophies and forces.

Please add my name to your newsletter list.

_____
name

_____
address

_____
city, state, zip

☐ I'm enclosing a tax-deductible donation for your work.